IMISCOE Research Series

Now accepted for Scopus! Content available on the Scopus site in spring 2021.

This series is the official book series of IMISCOE, the largest network of excellence on migration and diversity in the world. It comprises publications which present empirical and theoretical research on different aspects of international migration. The authors are all specialists, and the publications a rich source of information for researchers and others involved in international migration studies. The series is published under the editorial supervision of the IMISCOE Editorial Committee which includes leading scholars from all over Europe. The series, which contains more than eighty titles already, is internationally peer reviewed which ensures that the book published in this series continue to present excellent academic standards and scholarly quality. Most of the books are available open access.

Sabrina Marchetti

Migration and Domestic Work

IMISCOE Short Reader

 Springer

Sabrina Marchetti
Department of Philosophy and Cultural Heritage
Ca' Foscari University of Venice
Venezia, Italy

Ca' Foscari University of Venice, Dept of Philosophy and Cultural Heritage

ISSN 2364-4087   ISSN 2364-4095   (electronic)
IMISCOE Research Series
ISBN 978-3-031-11465-6   ISBN 978-3-031-11466-3   (eBook)
https://doi.org/10.1007/978-3-031-11466-3

This Springer imprint is published by the registered company Springer Nature Switzerland AG
The registered company address is: Gewerbestrasse 11, 6330 Cham, Switzerland

This publication has received funding from the European Research Council (ERC) under the European Union's Horizon 2020 Research and Innovation Programme, Grant Agreement n. 678783 (DomEQUAL).

Contents

About the Author

Prof Sabrina Marchetti is Associate Professor of Sociology at Ca' Foscari University of Venice. She specializes in issues of gender, racism, labour and migration, with a focus on the question of migrant domestic work. She has done extensive work as research consultant for NGOs, institutions and other research centres. She is an active member of several research networks working at a European level, among them the Research Network for Domestic Workers' Rights.

Abbreviations

ATRH	Association of Paid Domestic Workers (Ecuador)
C189	Convention No. 189 concerning Decent Work for Domestic Workers
FENATRAD	National Federation of Domestic Workers (Brazil)
GFMD	Global Forum on Migration and Development
IDWF	International Domestic Workers' Federation
ILO	International Labour Organization
ITUC	International Trade Union Confederation
UTRASD	Afro-Colombian Domestic Workers' Trade Union (Colombia)
WIEGO	Women in Informal Employment Globalizing and Organizing

List of Boxes

Chapter 1
Introduction

1.1 The Scope of This Book

This book wants to offer a systematic, rich and clear overview of the international debate on the importance of paid domestic and care work in contemporary migrations, as it has taken shape in the last 20 years. As will emerge in the following pages, the employment of migrant women in home-based care and cleaning work offers a paradigmatic example of the strong interlinkages between phenomena relating to gender, labour and migration, at the individual and collective levels.

Data from the International Labour Organization (ILO, 2015) has estimated the number of migrants who work as cleaners or care workers in other people's private households at 11.5 million; 73% of these are women or girls. These estimates attest to the importance of domestic and care work as a key to employment for women at the global level. This labour sector is particularly important in countries where the female population leaves to take up domestic work abroad, as is the case especially in Asia-Pacific countries, Eastern Europe and South America. Speaking of migration and domestic work also means that we have to elaborate on the reasons why, in wealthier and industrialized countries, increasing numbers of migrants are employed by private households in the sectors of childcare and elder care (Cox & Busch, 2018; Giles et al., 2014; Gottfried & Chun, 2018; Michel & Peng, 2017). The origins of these workers are very diverse: workers from the Philippines and Indonesia go mainly to other Asian countries, the Middle East, Europe or North America. For Eastern Europe, important origin countries are Ukraine, Romania and Moldova. Poland is at the same time both a country of origin (for women going to Germany and Western Europe) and a destination, especially for Ukrainians. In South or Central America, as well as in several African countries, we find mainly internal or South-South migrations. India is an interesting case, both as a locus of internal migration and as a sending country, with especially large numbers of women going

© The Author(s) 2022
S. Marchetti, *Migration and Domestic Work*, IMISCOE Research Series,
https://doi.org/10.1007/978-3-031-11466-3_1

to the Middle East.[1] In all these cases of international migration, phenomena related to domestic work overlap with different politics and systems of governance of migration, which vary from country to country, and over time.

In order to delve into the nexus between gender, migration and labour mentioned above, in this book I will explore four different dimensions of the experience of migrant domestic workers and related academic debates. First of all, I will describe the debate around care and domestic tasks, their importance in society, their political and economic organization, and the role of migrant women in the transnational industry that surrounds this unique market. Secondly, I will focus on the migration dimension, highlighting in particular the relevance of state policies in creating conditions of precarity and irregularity for domestic workers. However, the role of private actors such as agencies and intermediaries will also be considered. The following chapter will use an intersectional perspective to look at the inequalities and divisions that affect the experiences of migrant domestic workers, especially in their relationships with employers. The impact of economic (and health) crises will be also discussed in this chapter, as this puts further burdens on migrant domestic workers' labour and living conditions. Finally, the book includes a shorter chapter about the question of labour rights for domestic workers, providing examples of strategies and campaigns conducted by migrant domestic workers (and their allies) in this respect.

1.2   What Is Domestic Work?

In this book I talk about migrants who are paid 'domestic workers' – also increasingly called 'household workers'. But who are these workers? Broadly speaking, domestic workers provide personal and household care in the frame of a formal or informal employment relationship, which means that they work for one or more households (not their own) for a wage. Occupations and tasks considered to be domestic work vary across countries: they may cook; clean; do the laundry; iron; take care of children, adults, the elderly and the disabled; tend to the garden or pets; or drive the family car. They may work part-time, full-time or on an hourly basis, and may or may not live in the home of the employer.

However, domestic work is defined according to the workplace, which is the private household. Indeed, the defining feature of the work is exclusion from the labour rights and protections seen in other settings. As I will discuss, the private character of the employers (families, not businesses) and the space of the home (seen as a private matter), in addition to other aspects, such as the difficulty of measuring the outcomes of some of the tasks involved, are central elements that bring about the discrimination in these jobs.

---

[1] Recent overviews and discussions of the phenomenon of international migration in domestic and care work can be found in Cox & Busch, 2018; Gottfried & Chun, 2018; Giles et al., 2014; Michel & Peng, 2017.

The use of the term 'domestic work' proposed here is consistent with the definition adopted by the International Labour Organization which defines domestic work as 'work performed *in* and *for* the household', as in the Domestic Workers Convention No. 189, adopted in 2011.[2] The ILO definition is an attempt to bring together the very large variety of forms of domestic work that exists around the world. This usage is also consistent with the language used by the global domestic workers' movement, providing a common English translation for the various local terms used in the different national contexts (see among others: ILO, 2013: 7). However, I am aware that the definition is not entirely accepted by local domestic workers' organizations in all contexts. For instance, in India domestic workers' organizations favour narrowing down the definition to work performed *in* the household and not *for* the household. This is because the conditions of the almost entirely female workforce based in the house (for instance, cooking and cleaning), are very different to those of the largely male workforce of gardeners and drivers. As such, the groups do not organize jointly (Agarwala & Saha, 2018).

The scholarship on paid domestic work builds on the feminist debate that has used many different terms to cover the labour that is performed in the household, and has connected it to its larger function of 'reproduction'. The feminist debate that is most relevant to our discussion is the one on reproductive labour. In the 1960s, feminist scholars in different countries concentrated their attention on what they called reproductive labour with the aim of shedding light on the specificity of women's oppression within the political economy of capitalist societies (Barbagallo & Federici, 2012). They defined reproductive labour as the material and relational work necessary for the creation and re-creation of the workforce through time. Such work includes all activities aimed at the wellbeing and survival of societies, in particular care tasks relating to the nurturing, tending and assistance of children and of sick people, as well as the performance of housekeeping chores such as cleaning, cooking, and washing, that benefit all household members. It might be seen as the ensemble of tasks functional to people's prosperous living, day after day and across generations, at the material and symbolic level (Petersen, 2003).

This reproductive labour has historically been a normative obligation for women, in opposition to the assignment of productive labour to men (that is, work for the production of material goods). This dichotomy has been reinforced by moral and religious views that emphasize women's supposedly natural aptitude and skill in this realm, a realm traditionally considered inferior to men's sphere of activity. Challenging these assumptions, feminists have long argued for the valorization of reproductive labour within capitalist economies (Larguía & Dumoulin, 1976; Pateman, 1988; Picchio, 1992). Many women around the world have campaigned for recognition of the value of these activities, not only in social terms but to acknowledge the economic contribution that they make to society, and thus the way they are exploited in capitalist economies (Sarti et al., 2018). One outcome of this

---

[2] The full text of the convention is available here: https://www.ilo.org/dyn/normlex/en/f?p=NORMLEXPUB:12100:0::NO::P12100_ILO_CODE:C189

movement is the transnational Wages for Housework campaign. It was inspired, among others, by Silvia Federici, Mariarosa Dalla Costa and Selma James, and animated dozens of groups in Italy and the US (Dalla Costa & James, 1975; Federici, 1975; Gissi, 2018; Toupin, 2014).

Over the years, some scholars within the feminist debate have preferred to use the term 'care', which draws attention to the emotional aspects of this work, and to the needs of children, the ageing and the ill (Mahon & Robinson, 2011; Williams, 2011). The transition from a conception of care as a mainly familial relationship involving mostly women in unpaid work, towards a conception of care as a commodity, has made feminist economists speak of a care economy: a specific form of economy which differs substantially from others, given the intimate and personalized character of the service provided (Folbre, 2001; Zelizer, 2009). The term 'care economy' highlights an important shift: in traditional economies, care tasks were accomplished – almost in their totality – inside the household by (unpaid) female family members. In contemporary economies however, these activities are increasingly being commodified through an accelerating and seemingly unstoppable process. New intimate tasks, particularly those related to different types of body-work, are continually being incorporated into the market (Boris & Parreñas, 2010; Wolkowitz, 2006).

However, authors have also warned against this emphasis on care as a substitutive term for what was called reproductive work in previous literature. Eleonore Kofman, in particular, considers care a quite narrow concept, and still prefers to use the more powerful notion of social reproduction in order to explain the relationship between gender, migration and globalization despite the criticisms that the concept of reproduction has received in the past. In her view, the globalization of social reproduction is sufficient to explain the interconnection between what happens in a wider 'landscape of activities and sites' (Kofman, 2012). It is indeed important not to lose sight of the wider field within which the labour migration of domestic and care workers is taking place. For example, increasing numbers of women also migrate for marriage: whether these are wives reuniting with their husbands and children, or foreign spouses marrying Western men who are strangers, this migration ultimately serves the reproduction of families and societies on a transnational scale (Douglass, 2006). For Kofman (2012), only when speaking of the 'globalization of social reproduction' can we understand the linkages between apparently different phenomena such as migration for domestic, care and sex work, international adoption, migrants sending remittances to their countries of origin, pensioners settling in low-income countries to save resources, and households who opt to send children abroad for study to increase their cultural capital (see also Constable, 2016; Douglass, 2006).

Such issues have been made particularly relevant by the crisis of welfare states and the intensification of different forms of commodification of reproductive labour, which became visible in most industrialized countries at the beginning of the 1990s. In fact, during this time, with the beginning of a crisis of welfare state systems, the 'return to the family' of care previously taken up by the state provoked the expansion of a market of home-based care work. This is because families had not (or not fully) re-entered into the traditional care model, but had instead begun outsourcing at least part of their care commitments.

This leads me to the social stratification of workers in this sector, which establishes hierarchies between migrants along nationality, class and gender lines, contributing to their differential inclusion in the labour market. Migrant women are disadvantaged by policies privileging skilled migration as well as by legislation denying work permits to those who have migrated to reunite with their families. The ways in which these racialized and gendered representations inform the organization of domestic and care labour have attracted considerable scholarly attention, prompting research into the notion of a 'cultural' predisposition for care among women (and men) of certain nationalities (Gallo & Scrinzi, 2016; Lan, 2006; Marchetti, 2014). This stratification exacerbates the under-valuation of these jobs – as far as they are considered 'naturally' assigned to the most vulnerable and stigmatized subjects in each context (Gutiérrez-Rodríguez, 2010).

1.3   Women, Migration and Globalization

Domestic and care work offer a highly feminized scenario: women form the bulk of the care receivers, women are the paid caregivers and women are often the employers who organize this care provision. This tendency is due to the convergence of different highly gender-biased phenomena, namely the higher percentage of women among longer-living elderly people, the higher percentage of women among those who work in the care sector (in nursing homes as well as in hospitals and private homes) and finally the higher percentage of women among those who employ these workers, as family members or company managers responsible for the provision of care. In this book, I will focus mainly on one aspect of this feminized setting, namely the perspectives of workers, and to a lesser extent, those of their employers. Since women are usually both the employer and the employee in this sector, a situation often arises in which two women share an everyday, intimate, personal relationship directed at the accomplishment of highly gendered tasks, and yet they are positioned hierarchically.

The importance of care, domestic and sex work for the employment of all women through history is widely acknowledged (Hoerder et al., 2015; Schrover & Yeo, 2011). Speaking of the predominance of women in the care workforce, scholars have use the expression 'feminization of care' (Zelizer 2009) and have discussed the social factors behind this bias at length, as for example in Beverly Skeggs's (1997) analysis of the way in which the socialization of British working-class girls led them to seek employment in the care sector, or as Evelyn Nakano-Glenn (2002) and Nancy Folbre (2012) have demonstrated for US women. However, it is not class or gender alone that influences women's trajectories into domestic and care work as a paid occupation. These occupations have also historically been characterized by the strong presence of migrant and racialized people. Speaking about the US, Judith Rollins (1985) stresses that the employment of free or enslaved servants for care and cleaning chores goes back a long way in history. Dirk Hoerder (2011) examines the formation of a racialized 'serving class' composed of enslaved women as early as the eighteenth century. Indeed, the present-day composition of the workforce employed in the sector continues to result from the intertwining of multiple processes of marginalization, along context-specific dimensions of social inequality. As a result, domestic workers usually belong to the most impoverished and socially stigmatized groups: migrants, low-caste people, rural, black and indigenous women, and so on, depending on the context (Marchetti et al., 2021). Moreover, their situation across countries is strongly influenced by the multidimensional transformations brought about by globalization, due in particular to the intensification of international migration.

In fact, as Eleonore Kofman and Parvati Raghuram say, 'global transformations are also gendered transformations… gender is an important factor influencing migration today' (Kofman & Raghuram, 2015: 11). Along the same lines, Laura Oso and Natalia Ribas-Mateos (2013) describe two dimensions in which gender is ingrained in the organization of global migrations. On the one hand, we see that women and men are differently employed at the sites where industrial production has been delocalized from the centre to the peripheries. Indeed, the international division of industrial production shows gender-segregated sectors of employment, with women and girls more often working in what Bridget Anderson (2000) calls the 3D jobs: dangerous, demanding and demeaning. This tendency was already clear in 1984 when Mirjana Morokvašic wrote that the 'women from the peripheral zones … represent a ready-made labour supply which is, at once, the most vulnerable, the most flexible and … the least demanding workforce [in terms of rights]' (Morokvašic, 1984: 886). Such gender-based differentiation affects peripheral migrations from impoverished regions towards nearby areas where newly delocalized production demands their labour (Enloe, 1989). An example of this is the employment in industrialized countries of migrant women and men for distinct types of work: migrant men in construction, mining or the metal industry; migrant women in textiles, electronics and the food industry. Both women and men are employed in agricultural work, including work on a seasonal basis.

On the other hand, gender is also relevant to global migration when we look at what happens in advanced industrialized countries. Such countries become receivers of migrant workers for all the sectors that are not (yet) delocalized and that demand cheap and flexible labour. Importantly, these include 'domestic service, catering, personal and sex work [that] cannot be exported in the same way as industrial activity' (Oso & Ribas-Mateos, 2013: 10), and where migrant women are disproportionately employed. Following on, Saskia Sassen (2000), Thanh-Dam Truong (1996) and Oso and Ribas-Mateos (2013) thus identify a second channel of the North–South transfer of work that runs parallel, although in the opposite direction, to the one described above for agro-industrial labour.

In 2001, Rhacel Parreñas introduced the phrase 'the international division of reproductive labour' to expand the view from its 'racial' division (Nakano-Glenn, 2002) to the global level. Parreñas finds it important to emphasize how this work tends to be unequally distributed along a 'three-tier transfer of reproductive labour in globalization between the following groups of women: (1) middle-class women in receiving nations, (2) migrant domestic workers, and (3) Third World women who are too poor to migrate' (Parreñas, 2001: 560). In her study on the Filipino diaspora, she found that the same Filipino women employed in Western households to care for children and the elderly are delegating their own family commitments to other women: other female family members, but also other women from poorer backgrounds, to whom they pay a salary of about USD 40 per month out of the USD 1000 they earn abroad – for doing the same job (Parreñas 2005). In this view, globalization is the background against which reproductive work is divided up and passed on from one woman to another, less privileged, woman.

The same idea has been taken up by Arlie Russell Hochschild, who uses the catchier expression 'global care chain' to suggest the existence of a bond between women from different parts of the world who have to come to terms with the care duties placed on their shoulders by gender inequality. For Hochschild, this produces a 'care drain' from the Global South to the Global North due to the 'the importation of care and love from poor countries to rich ones' (Hochschild, 2002: 17). It is important to notice how, in her view, the focus is no longer on reproduction generally, but on a specific ingredient of reproductive labour: love, which she sees as an 'unfairly distributed resource – extracted from one place and enjoyed somewhere else' (Hochschild, 2002: 22). In the wake of Hochschild's argument on 'care drain', a plethora of studies has explored the question of the lack of attention suffered by the children of international migrant women (Parreñas, 2005; Pratt, 2012).

1.4   A Multi-layered Approach

This book will delve into the experiences of migrant domestic workers as part of the larger process of feminization of migration. In particular, I will use the notions of 'international division of reproductive labour' (Parreñas, 2001) and 'global care chains' (Hochschild, 2002) to emphasize the inequality in the way care and domestic tasks are today distributed between middle-class women in receiving nations and migrant domestic workers (Parreñas, 2001).

However, the nexus between migration and domestic work also demands a more multi-layered approach. The conditions of these migrant workers, being mainly women, are shaped by the intersection of three different political regimes, as described by Helma Lutz (2011). As far as the *migration regime* is concerned, state policies strongly influence the employment of migrants for care and domestic work (Anderson & Ruhs, 2010). It has been noted how migration policies are crucial for understanding the large numbers of undocumented migrants who work in house cleaning, elder care, catering and restaurants (Ong, 1999; Triandafyllidou, 2016). In this regard, several studies have paid special attention to the question of citizenship and the legal rights of migrant domestic workers: Raffaella Sarti (2005) provides a historical and comparative analysis of the evolution of their legal status, while scholars like Rhacel Parreñas (2001), Encarnación Gutierrez Rodriguez (2010),

Abigail Bakan and Daiva Stasiulis (1994) talk about the implications of their condition as undocumented or 'partial citizens' in Europe and the US.

In relation to the *gender regime*, it is important to consider the relevance of care, domestic and sex work for the employment of all women, not only migrants (Boris & Parreñas, 2010; Hoerder et al., 2015; Oso & Ribas-Mateos, 2013). I use concepts developed by the feminist scholars who have defined all these tasks (whether paid or unpaid) as 'reproductive labour' or 'social reproduction'. The employment of migrant women in such jobs can be seen as part of a growing process wherever new intimate tasks are being commodified, resulting in a precarious workforce with strong gender, race, class-based connotations (Sassen, 2002; Wolkowitz, 2006).

Finally, concerning the *welfare regime*, we know that different welfare systems with a multitude of care arrangements and 'care markets', lead to different types of migration (Ambrosini, 2013; Da Roit & Weicht, 2013; Van Hooren, 2012). Scholars distinguish between various combinations, such those of familistic care regimes which may produce 'migrant in the family' care models, and liberal regimes leading to 'migrant in the market' models. For example, in Europe, since public nurseries, homes for the elderly and hospitals can no longer satisfy the demands made on them, families have shifted to purchasing market-based care and cleaning services (see Triandafyllidou & Marchetti, 2015).

We also know that welfare models do not only depend on state policies but are also sustained by a specific 'culture of care' and mindset which favours certain practices over others. Hiring an external person, especially if that person is a migrant, is not always well regarded or supported by households and their social networks. This also relates to specific views on women's role in the family, concerns about parenting models, and visions of the life of the elderly and illness. Thus, with reference to Helma Lutz's delineation of the three regimes mentioned above, it is important to speak of the conjunction between the welfare regime and the gender regime and how they set normative frameworks in relation to family life and care needs.

Indeed the intertwining of these three different regimes explains the imbalance affecting the distribution of reproductive tasks between people: from a gender perspective, women do take up a bigger share than their male counterparts; but it is also true that *between* women, reproductive work is more often done by black or migrant women, and generally by women from minority and racialized groups (Nakano-Glenn, 2002; Palmer, 1989; Rollins, 1985). In most industrialized countries, it has been noted that looking at the condition of citizenship is crucial to understanding the specific discrimination experienced by the large numbers of undocumented migrants (mostly women, but also men) who work in house cleaning, elderly care, catering and restaurants. The private employment of domestic and care workers in particular, is negatively affected by existing migration policies that make the regular employment of migrants difficult (Ong, 1999; Triandafyllidou, 2016). In the next chapter, we will move on to a discussion on how these different regimes intertwine in the social and economic organization of care and reproductive work.

References

Agarwala, R., & Saha, S. (2018). The employment relationship and movement strategies among domestic Workers in India. *Critical Sociology, 44*(7–8), 1207–1223.

Ambrosini, M. (2013). *Irregular migration and invisible welfare*. Palgrave Macmillan.

Anderson, B. (2000). *Doing the dirty work? The global politics of domestic labour*. Zed Books.

Anderson, B., & Ruhs, M. (2010). Researching illegality and labour migration. *Population, Space and Place, 16*(3), 175–179.

Bakan, A. B., & Stasiulis, D. (1994). Foreign domestic worker policy in Canada and the social boundaries of modern citizenship. *Science and Society 58*(1), 7–33.

Barbagallo, C., & Federici, S. (2012). Introduction to 'care work' and the commons. *Commoner, 15*, 1–21.

Boris, E., & Parreñas, R. S. (Eds.). (2010). *Intimate labors: Cultures, technologies, and the politics of care*. Stanford University Press.

Constable, N. (2016). Reproductive labor at the intersection of three intimate industries: Domestic work, sex tourism, and adoption. *Positions, 24*, 45–69.

Cox, R., & Busch, N. (2018). *As an equal?: Au pairing in the 21st century*. Zed Books.

Da Roit, B., & Weicht, B. (2013). Migrant care work and care, migration and employment regimes. *Journal of European Social Policy, 23*(5), 469–486.

Dalla Costa, M., & James, S. (1975). *The power of women and the subversion of the community*. Falling Wall Press.

Douglass, M. (2006). Global householding in Pacific Asia. *International Development Planning Review, 28*, 421–445.

Enloe, C. (1989). *Bananas, beaches and bases*. Pandora Press.

Federici, S. (1975). *Wages against housework*. Falling Wall.

Folbre, N. (2001). *The invisible heart: Economics and family values*. New Press.

Folbre, N. (2012). *For love and money*. Sage.

Gallo, E., & Scrinzi, F. (2016). *Migration, masculinities and reproductive labour: Men of the home*. Springer.

Giles, P. W., Preston, P. V., & Romero, P. M. (2014). *When care work goes global: Locating the social relations of domestic work*. Ashgate.

Gissi, A. (2018). The home as a factory: Rethinking the debate on housewives' wages in Italy, 1929–1980. In R. Sarti, A. Bellavitis, & M. Martini (Eds.), *What is work? Gender at the cross-roads of home, family, and business from the early modern era to the present* (pp. 152–177). Berghahn Books.

Gottfried, H., & Chun, J. J. (2018). Care work in transition: Transnational circuits of gender, migration, and care. *Critical Sociology, 44*(7–8), 997–1012.

Gutiérrez-Rodríguez, E. (2010). *Migration, domestic work and affect: A Decolonial approach on value and the feminization of labour*. Routledge.

Hochschild, A. (2002). Love and gold. In B. Ehrenreich & A. Hochschild (Eds.), *Global woman: Nannies, maids, and sex workers in the new economy* (pp. 15–30). Henry Holt.

Hoerder, D. (2011). From one black Atlantic to many: Slave regimes, creole societies, and power relationships in the Atlantic world. In D. R. Gabaccía & D. Hoerder (Eds.), *Connecting seas and Connected Ocean rims: Indian, Atlantic, and Pacific oceans and China seas migrations from the 1830s to the 1930s* (pp. 258–280). Brill.

Hoerder, D., Van Nederveen, E., & Neunsinger, S. (2015). *Towards a global history of domestic and caregiving workers*. Brill.

ILO. (2013). *Domestic workers across the world: Global and regional statistics and the extent of legal protection*. ILO.

ILO. (2015). *Global estimates of migrant workers and migrant domestic workers: Results and methodology*. ILO.

Kofman, E. (2012). Gendered labour migrations in Europe and emblematic migratory figures. *Journal of Ethnic and Migration Studies, 39*(4), 579–600.

Kofman, E., & Raghuram, P. (2015). *Gendered migrations and global social reproduction*. Palgrave Macmillan.

Lan, P. C. (2006). *Global Cinderellas: Migrant domestic and newly rich employers in Taiwan*. Duke University Press.

Larguía, I., & Dumoulin, J. (1976). *Hacia una ciencia de la liberación de la Mujer*. Anagrama.

Lutz, H. (2011). *The new maids: Transnational women and the care economy*. Zed Books.

Mahon, R., & Robinson, F. (2011). *Feminist ethics and social policy: Towards a new global political economy of care*. UBC Press.

Marchetti, S. (2014). *Black girls: Migrant domestic workers and colonial legacies*. Brill.

Marchetti, S., Cherubini, D., & Garofalo Geymonat, G. (2021). *Global domestic workers: Intersectional inequalities and struggles for rights*. Bristol UP.

Michel, S., & Peng, I. (2017). *Gender, migration, and the work of care: A multi-scalar approach to the Pacific rim*. Springer.

Morokvaśic, M. (1984). Birds of passage are also women. *International Migration Review, 18*, 886–907.

Nakano-Glenn, E. (2002). *Unequal freedom: How race and gender shaped American citizenship and labor*. Harvard University Press.

Ong, A. (1999). *Flexible citizenship: The cultural logics of Transnationality*. Duke University Press.

Oso, L., & Ribas-Mateos, N. (2013). *The international handbook on gender, migration and transnationalism*. Edward Elgar Publishing.

Palmer, P. (1989). *Domesticity and dirt: Housewives and domestic servants in the United States, 1920–1945*. Temple University Press.

Parreñas, R. S. (2001). *Servants of globalization: Women, migration and domestic work*. Stanford University Press.

Parreñas, R. S. (2005). *Children of global migration: Transnational families and gendered woes*. Stanford University Press.

Pateman, C. (1988). *The sexual contract*. Stanford University Press.

Petersen, S. V. (2003). *A critical rewriting of global political economy: Integrating reproductive, productive and virtual economies*. Routledge.

Picchio, A. (1992). *Social reproduction: The political economy of the labour market*. Cambridge University Press.

Pratt, L. (2012). *Families apart: Migrant mothers and the conflicts of labor and love*. University of Minnesota Press.

Rollins, J. (1985). *Between women: Domestics and their employers*. Temple University Press.

Sarti, R. (2005). Freedom and citizenship? The legal status of servants and domestic workers in a comparative perspective (16th–21st centuries). In S. Pasleau & I. Schopp (Eds.), *Proceedings of the servant project* (Vol. 3, pp. 127–164).

Sarti, R., Bellavitis, A., & Martini, M. (Eds.). (2018). *What is work? Gender at the crossroads of home, family, and business from the early modern era to the present*. Berghahn.

Sassen, S. (2000). Women's burden: Counter-geographies of globalization and the feminization of survival. *Journal of International Affairs, 53*, 503–524.

Sassen, S. (2002). Global cities and survival circuits. In B. Ehrenreich & A. R. Hochschild (Eds.), *Global woman: Nannies, maids and sex workers in the new economy* (pp. 254–274). Granta Books.

Schrover, M., & Yeo, E. (2011). *Gender, migration, and the public sphere, 1850–2005*. Routledge.

Skeggs, B. (1997). *Formations of class and gender: Becoming respectable*. Sage.

Toupin, L. (2014). Le Salaire au Travail Menager: Chronique d'une lutte féministe internationale (1972–1977). *Montréal: les éditions du remue-ménage*.

Triandafyllidou, A. (2016). *Irregular migrant domestic Workers in Europe: Who cares?* Routledge.

Triandafyllidou, A., & Marchetti, S. (Eds.). (2015). *Employers, agencies and immigration: Care work in Europe*. Ashgate.

Truong, T.-D. (1996). Gender, international migration and social reproduction: Implications for theory, policy, research and networking. *Asian and Pacific Migration Journal, 5*, 27–52.

Van Hooren, F. (2012). Varieties of migrant care work: Comparing patterns of migrant labour in social care. *Journal of European Social Policy, 22*(2), 133–147.

Williams, F. (2011). Towards a transnational analysis of the political economy of care. In R. Mahon & F. Robinson (Eds.), *Feminist ethics and social policy: Towards a new global political economy of care* (pp. 21–38). UBC Press.

Wolkowitz, C. (2006). *Bodies at work*. Sage.

Zelizer, V. (2009). *The purchase of intimacy*. Princeton University Press.

Chapter 2
Care and Domestic Work

2.1 Not Just Another Job

The transnational migration of women (and some men) as domestic and care workers is based on the increasing expansion of a private market which is recruiting
workers, mainly in the Global South, to perform tasks relating to reproductive
labour in wealthier countries. To understand the experience of these workers, it is
important to consider how this labour market differs from others. It cannot be
reduced to payment for the performance of tasks. It is also undoubtedly affected by
the private realm in which it takes place. Some scholars have argued that the uniqueness of this labour market lies in the intimacy that it is charged with, as a consequence of the physicality of care work, the privacy of the domestic setting in which
it takes place, and the relevance of the interpersonal dimension it entails (Parreñas
& Boris, 2010). Let us look more closely at these different elements.

Firstly, it's worth stressing that the content of the work – what is 'sold' – is a
matter open for discussion. For some authors, workers are not simply offering the
accomplishment of a task; they are 'selling a relationship'. For example, for Arlie
Russell Hochschild 'love' is actually what is sold here, the commodified object at
stake. We are confronted with an important example of what she calls 'emotional
work' (Hochschild, 2012). For Hochschild, taking care of someone falls into a category of jobs based on a process of 'outsourcing of the self', meaning that care
receivers expect their caregivers to be able to materialize their wishes, to understand
those wishes and make them a reality (Hochschild, 2012). This can range from
being tended to and assisted in the proper way, to receiving a nice meal and good
company. As Encarnacion Gutiérrez-Rodríguez (2010) explains with reference to
affect theories, these tasks equally affect the person who performs them and those
who benefit from their performance. The activist for domestic workers' rights
Ai-Jen Poo also emphasizes the importance of caregivers' capacity to provide emotional support to ageing people as something which needs more recognition (Poo &
Conrad, 2009).

© The Author(s) 2022   13
S. Marchetti, *Migration and Domestic Work*, IMISCOE Research Series,
https://doi.org/10.1007/978-3-031-11466-3_2

As mentioned in the previous chapter, feminist sociologists such as Carol Wolkowitz (2006) have specifically reflected on the physical dimension of this type of work which is fundamentally based on bodily contact, as is the case for many other jobs performed by women in the health, care and service sector more generally. Such body work is usually associated with menial and strenuous jobs relating to cleaning, tending children, the elderly and sick people. In this perspective, such body-to-body work is very different from work done by machines or even work that entails human contact but not physical touching. Thus, it is very intensive work that demands not only physical strength but also attentiveness, emotional responsiveness and endurance, therefore putting workers at risk at both the physical and psychological level.

Therefore, the importance of the home as a very special place of employment emerges. In their interactions, workers and employers have to continuously renegotiate the boundaries between their working and personal lives. It is useful to examine this through the lens of feminist arguments on domesticity and the politization of the public-private dichotomy (Davidoff, 2003). It is in this 'politicized' domestic space that the relationship between migrant domestic workers and their employers can be interpreted: for instance, by looking at the way the domestic and care practices delegated from employers to workers are regulated by division along class, gender and racial lines, and therefore organized along axes of power. The home is thus the site where identities are shaped, contested, and reshaped over time. Similarly, Yeoh and Huang (1999) see homes where migrant domestic workers are employed as 'contact zones', while Janet Momsen (1999) talks about 'culture-contact situations'. Homes are very much shaped by national culture and identities. Blunt and Dowlings (2006) talk about homes in which discourses and practices related to nationhood are reproduced. In what they refer to as 'lived and metaphorical experiences of home', people create a sense of identity that then calls for an analysis of the power relations that make the home an 'intensely political' site.

In view of this relationship, I consider the home not simply as a 'space', but rather as a 'place', that is, a specific location where subjects' experience takes shape. The difference between space and place is emphasized by Doreen Massey, who defines a place as the result of particular interactions and of social relationships which occur in that specific location (Massey, 1994). For this reason, when looking at the interactions between employers and employees in the domestic sphere, one should see a place rather than a space, as it is a specific location where different forces interact. The domestic place where these encounters occur, practically and metaphorically, reflects the structure of the social space, where different subjects occupy a range of positions. In this view, the organization of these homes as workplaces is crossed by boundaries separating the middle and upper class in opposition to the working class, and European citizens versus migrant (often undocumented) workers. In fact, I consider these homes as crucial places where we can observe what has been called 'everyday bordering', with reference to the fact that an anti-migration attitude is not only about patrolling physical borders to reject migrants, but is also concerned with enacting separations between migrants and non-migrants in their everyday encounters, such at the workplace, hospitals or schools

(Yuval-Davis et al., 2019). When it comes to migrant domestic workers, private homes, as simultaneously their accommodation and workplace, are fraught with difficulties.

2.2 The Care Economy Debate

As we have seen, towards the end of the 1990s, scholars started to talk about the specificities of the market surrounding care and reproductive work once these became commodities, that is, like goods that can be sold and exchanged. Vivian Zelizer (2009) uses the expression 'economy of care' to refer to the specific market created by the delegation to others of tasks otherwise understood as private and intimate. The process of commodification of care has increasingly intensified through the years, investing more and more activities (performed both in private homes, hospitals and other residential facilities) and drawing on a growing workforce which, as mentioned, includes large numbers of migrant women.

An important author in this debate is Claire Ungerson. In 1997, she defined this process of commodification of care as the 'marketization of intimacy'. She described how, while in traditional economies the bulk of reproductive tasks was accomplished inside the household by (unpaid) female family members, in contemporary economies these activities are increasingly available on the market, from meals prepared by professional cooks that can be bought in restaurants, to the fact that elderly people can be assisted by paid caregivers in nursing homes.

This leads her to say that 'the commodification of care exists and is growing; we have yet to develop an adequate understanding of its implications for citizens, carers, and users' (Ungerson, 1997, p. 379). Importantly, Ungerson questions the meaning of this commodification process for our understanding of the nexus between care and gendered citizenship. She is concerned that 'the presence of money' will affect the nature of care relationships. Different views on differences based on class, race, and gender may also play a role in such labour markets (Ungerson, 1997, p. 379).

Other authors have highlighted the peculiar functioning of the care market: not a market in which goods are produced and exchanged, but a market based on service provision, where what is sold are 'relational services'. This view of care and domestic work as a service has a number of consequences and limitations. For example, for Susan Eaton it was difficult for caregivers to quantify in their bills 'the time to listen to somebody's story, time to hold their hand, time to comfort somebody who is feeling trouble' (Eaton, 1996: 7). In a similar perspective, Nicola Yeates (2004) makes a distinction between 'caring for' and 'caring about' to indicate the limits to commodifying care. If it is possible to quantify the work needed to care for something, it is more difficult to quantify (and require payment) for the work involved in caring 'about' someone. Indeed, the extent of commodification is constrained by the type of care labour involved ('caring about' not being amenable to commodification) as well as by cultural norms. Anna Yeatman (2009) is critical about thinking of care as a service, since it is extremely hard to produce an assessment or to appraise the 'output' of the care provided. The question is essentially whether those who buy these services should be seen more as 'customers' or as employers or patients. If the term 'employers' implies centrality of the working relationship, and 'patients' indicates that care and wellbeing are the primary focus; then 'customers' places ultimate importance on the service dimension: that is, the satisfaction of the client (Cranford & Miller, 2013).

Another key author in this debate is Nancy Folbre. Her main argument centres on the distinction between the unpaid care typically provided in the family setting, and the paid care provided in a working relationship. She highlights that while love is usually considered a proper intrinsic motivation to perform care tasks, money, by contrast, is seen as a suspicious extrinsic reason to engage in it (Folbre, 2012, pp. 22–4). For Folbre, this dichotomy between intrinsic and extrinsic motivations permeates the entire realm of care provision considered as a service, explaining the paradoxes and tensions experienced by caregivers and care receivers alike. With other terms, Viviane Zelizer (2009) has already said that in the realm of intimacy, love and money are constructed as two 'hostile worlds'.

Moreover, Folbre argues that the care market is not like other competitive service markets for a number of reasons. She argues that care jobs rely on trust as their fundamental element, and it is the collaborative relationship between all the people involved that determines the quality of the service (Folbre, 2012, p. 35–6). Care-managers should find a balance between controlling workers and giving them freedom to accomplish their tasks as they wish, in a spirit of mutual collaboration and discretion. At the same time, she also draws attention to the fact that care recipients are often not capable of expressing their own satisfaction. This subverts the assumptions about the 'consumer sovereignty' that usually dominates in both customer services and in personal care (Folbre, 2012, p. 3). Folbre considers the intimacy that surrounds the provision of care for children, elderly people and sick people an obstacle to an exact quantification of the 'cost' of this type of labour, which goes well beyond a clear-cut relationship between assignments and outputs (Folbre, 2012, 3). In fact, care provision is also influenced by what William Baumol (1967) described as a paradox when the wages of workers are not based on their productivity, but on external factors that influence the value of the labour (Simonazzi, 2011; Yeates, 2009).

To sum up, many scholars deem the expansion of care markets detrimental as long as it promotes a reductive understanding of 'both care as a commodity, and the individual in need of care as a consumer' (Anttonen & Haïkiö, 2011: 71). In fact, many authors are critical of a vision of care systems as based on individual decision-making, that is, considering care receivers to be customers that shop around and make choices concerning care services as they would when buying other types of products (Glendinning, 2008; Shutes & Walsh, 2012; Stevens et al., 2011). Along these lines, Catherine Needham highlights how the 'personalization' of services has become the main narrative underwriting the public service reforms carried out from the 1990s onwards that promoted the privatization of care provisions and its

> **Box 2.1: 'Care Debates' in Latin America**
>
> Among feminists in Latin American countries, debates on care and reproductive labour have generated new productive concepts. Care issues are often translated as 'economías feminista, social y solidaria', to include all social activities (paid and unpaid) that contribute to society, are based on principles of reciprocity, and that emphasize social interconnections (Quiroga Diaz, 2009). Care and reproductive labour are often understood in more general terms as something that ought to be pursued as a social value. Since this is embodied by women, they should be respected and valorised.
>
> Since the 1980s, feminist scholars in Latin America such as Mérola (1985) and Luz Gabriela Arango Gaviria (1997) have emphasized the question of reproductive labour. Another example is the special issue of *Iconos,* a journal edited by Vega and Gutiérrez Rodríguez (2014), with several contributions applying recent debates on care to different national contexts, like Claudia Fonseca and Jurema Brites's essay (2014) on Brazil, or Pascale Molinier and Luz Gabriela Arango Gaviria's (2014) work on Colombia.

outsourcing to non-state actors (Needham, 2011). Authors also warn against the easy dichotomy between unpaid care seen as rigid and inefficient, and paid care service seen as more flexible, efficient, and attentive to the needs of care receivers (Clarke, 2006). As I will discuss further in the following pages, this dichotomy tends to obscure the neoliberal shift by which citizens are turned into consumers, ultimately responsible for their own care needs, while states are limited to merely ensuring that private (care) markets work (Box 2.1).

2.3   A Transnational Care Industry

By adopting such a framework, we see how migrant care and domestic workers are increasingly filling the gaps in care provision in wealthier and industrialized societies through their (often irregular) jobs in the domestic sector and in care-related occupations. In other words, they are filling the gaps of what Fiona Williams (2011) defines as the 'transnational political economy of care'. This is a consequence of the fact that, as for example in Southern Europe, the increasing participation of women in the labour market has not brought about changes in the traditional division of roles within their families. Migrant women seem to substitute for local women in their traditional reproductive role. The old system of the gendered division of labour has simply been maintained or reproduced through a new supply of labour along racialized lines (Andall, 2000). In fact, as mentioned in Chap. 1, the international division of care work reveals the importance of the intersections between gender and other social categories, such as race/ethnicity, class, age, and so forth (Anthias

& Yuval-Davis, 1992; Guillaumin, 1997). Furthermore, we have seen how, since the new migratory flows are taking place in the context of increasingly fortified boundaries, this also means that in some contexts, domestic work is becoming one of the few available channels for regular migration for women. Studies have shown how the articulation of immigration policies with social policies creates a gendered and racialized division of labour (Gallo & Scrinzi, 2016; Lutz, 2008).

However, recent developments of scholarship in this field have highlighted the necessity of broadening this analysis by investigating other social actors who have a stake in the issue of migrant domestic labour. Up until this recent development, most studies have focused on the traditional forms of domestic service in the private sphere; by contrast, Eleonore Kofman (2012) stresses the importance of incorporating into the analysis other agents of social reproduction besides the household, such as the market and the non-profit sector. She points out how the international division of care takes shape in the care industry providing home-based services for the elderly. Such commodification of care work at the transnational level is considered to be responsible for increased levels of inequality and exploitation (Williams, 2011; Yeates, 2009).

In this view, Nicola Yeates (2004) discusses the private provision of various types of care work, emphasizing the importance of strengthening the linkages between the concepts of the 'global care chain' and the 'global commodity chain', at least at the theoretical level. The challenge, for Yeates, is to go beyond the case of migrant domestic and care workers, to look at more actors – especially corporate care providers – and forms of outsourced service work, depending on what prevails in each context and historical period. Expanding the analysis to the role of corporate providers seems useful in understanding growing phenomena such as the transnational recruitment of nurses and doctors due to the privatization of formerly public health and care services in industrialized countries which are now in search of a cheap, flexible and yet highly skilled workforce (Connell, 2008; Kingma, 2007; Näre & Nordberg, 2016; Yeates, 2004). Yeates further develops her argument, speaking about the emergence of a corporate care industry, with particular reference to the US. As she puts it:

> care corporations provide a range of personal health and social care services in institutional (hospitals, nursing homes, nurseries) and domestic (households) settings; house care corporations provide private households with various 'housewife' services and maintenance, pest control and repairs. Corporations may specialize in one of these types of services or may combine different types of services (e.g., personal and house care). (Yeates, 2004, 382).

Yeates sees 'the corporate care industry [as] a major area of economic growth and employment generation' (ibid.) in many countries, even though public and informal providers remain a significant source of less profitable and non-profitable care services. In summary, Yeates offers a broad concept of care corporatization, which includes a wide range of for-profit suppliers; from self-employed individuals, to small enterprises, to agencies and multinationals. Accordingly, she charts the differences between various corporate care actors in terms of their size and the reach of their commercial activities, from the sub-national to the national and international scales (Yeates, 2004, 382). In the next section, I highlight the kinds of imageries which are associated with such care arrangements.

2.4   Imageries of Care

In our article on the emerging corporatization of care, Sara Farris and I introduced the notion of 'imageries of care' to account for a further dimension of the various kinds of social organization of care on the basis of national differences, in this complex landscape (Farris & Marchetti, 2017). With this concept we wanted to tackle what ideas prevail concerning who is considered responsible for care provision and what responses are considered most suitable, in each context. A given group can be more inclined to think that care should be provided for free and organized by the state in institutional settings, while others may think that care is too intimate, and it can only go through a personal relationship, whether paid or paid, but certainly provided in personal and home-based forms.

Ideas such as the latter can be found in contexts where the familial model of care still prevails (Farris & Marchetti, 2017). At the practical level, we show how this model fails to take into account the concrete aspects concerning the modality, duration, and tasks of the assistance provided, in a one-to-one and very personal setting. Such imagery is associated with the realities of caregiving within family settings, mostly by female members, women and girls, in charge of fulfilling all reproductive tasks to support the entire household, notably taking care of children and elderly or sick relatives. Although one may think that this configuration is a legacy of the past, in our view this 'familial imagery of care' in fact still prevails today, even in settings where commodification is quite developed and caregivers are paid workers. In this situation, they are employed by the household of the care receiver and expected to offer a caring relationship which emulates the one existing between family members. As we will later see, this model has a strong influence on the employment experiences of many of the migrant women working in the transnational care market, especially in countries where a family-based social structure predominates.

At the opposite end of the spectrum of these ideal types of care imageries is the one we associate with the increasing marketization of care which, as Farris and I argue, may reach the point of a corporatization of care services (Farris & Marchetti, 2017). In these situations, care is understood as a highly structured activity, articulated in well-defined tasks with a specific duration and clear methods of provision. This type of imagery is spreading in national contexts where institutional residential homes are more common, or where home-based care is organized via agencies. In these care settings the one-to-one care relationship no longer prevails, since multiple caregivers rotate in shifts to attend to the same person. Their work is organized according to rigid schedules and forms of control, which makes it necessary to unpack complex activities into easily quantifiable tasks, to which the payment for these jobs corresponds. Such imagery is increasingly common in countries with ageing populations where the employment of caregivers is not directly managed by households, but rather via private agencies or public-private institutions. Therefore, as we say:

> by turning it into an activity that is ever more codified, less personalized, poorly paid and less sensitive to the changing needs of the people towards whom it is oriented … care work is becoming the contested territory for the penetration of new forms of capitalist restructuring (Farris & Marchetti, 2017, p. 127).

Such settings are becoming common for migrant workers, as long as these employment services continue to seek an increasingly qualified workforce through recruitment abroad, due simultaneously to the lack of a national workforce for these poorly paid and precarious jobs, and the increased demand for care in industrialized, ageing societies.

Exploring the difference in the imageries of care between countries, in Triandafyllidou and Marchetti (2015) we have identified some regional patterns across Europe. There is, first of all, a pattern typical of northern and post-soviet European countries where institutionalized care is preferred over home-based care. In this setting, the private employment of care and domestic workers is seen as a challenge to ideals of equality, exacerbating class differences between women (Kristensen, 2017; Radziwinowiczówna et al., 2018). By contrast, in southern European countries care is provided inside the home by family members, notably women. Here, deciding to delegate care work to another person is often experienced as a necessary practical arrangement, yet fraught with moral and emotional distress due to feelings of disappointing expectations of mothers, wives or daughters (Marchetti, 2015; Vega Solís, 2009). Similar patterns concerning the impact of the national culture of care on employment relationships can be found in countries outside Europe. Along the same lines, research has shown that employers' attitudes towards the delegation of care and domestic tasks are of paramount importance in shaping employment relationships, from South Africa (Galvaan et al., 2015) to Yemen (De Regt, 2009) and Singapore (Lundström, 2013).

Moreover, it is important to ask oneself whether the delegation of care work to others has itself changed the way care is understood. Already in 1997, Ungerson noted – on the basis of interviews with care receivers to the elderly – how the possibility of cash payments has changed their understanding of care to something that was not obvious, not 'for free' (Ungerson, 1997).

However, caregivers are not all the same. There is a division between the role of the paid worker as the one in charge of everyday face-to-face interactions (Folbre's 'interactive care'), and that of unpaid caregivers (usually a female relative) who care more generally for the physical and psychological wellbeing of the care recipient (Marchetti, 2015). Similar worker-employer relationships have been observed in the field of private childcare, where working mothers think of themselves as those in charge of the education and wellbeing of their children, although the everyday care tasks may be covered by a (migrant) woman in their employ (Anderson, 2000).

This corresponds to a transformation in the way we see the role of mothers, daughters, and so on in households that employ a private caregiver. As Cristina Vega Solís (2009) argues for Spain, the increase in paid forms of care work transformed the lives of the daughters of elderly parents, enabling them to delegate tasks that would traditionally be performed by themselves, so that they went from being caregivers to care managers. In Italy, Maurizio Ambrosini (2013) also emphasizes the crucial role of employers in paying the care worker's wages and discussing contractual conditions, regularizing the legal status of migrant employees (when they are undocumented), administering medicines and special treatments to the elderly, and providing instructions about meals, rest times and outings for the elderly individuals. In today's care arrangements, care managers require many skills to satisfy the needs of recipients, relying on any available public or private resources, and navigating the private market of domestic work and care work to employ a suitable caregiver (Marchetti, 2015). In this view, employers are indeed pivotal actors in setting the conditions of the rapidly expanding market economy which is developing around the care and domestic labour sector. Employers find themselves torn between the demands of the family and the market when assessing the care which is needed and the resources required; they either buy care or mobilize their own time and energy to provide it. In other words, there is a very thin line separating the role of these employers as family caregivers from that of market actors, since they can afford to delegate this same care-giving to a paid worker. In that case, employers have to juggle meagre welfare allowances or service provisions for the elderly or children with rising care needs (particularly of the elderly in Europe's ageing population), while women are increasingly engaged in full-time paid work outside the home (Triandafyllidou & Marchetti, 2015).

In Triandafyllidou and Marchetti (2015) we argued that employers of paid domestic workers may be classed into two main categories: employers as agents of social change, and employers as preservers of traditions. The first category includes employers such as the working mothers of young children or the daughters of elderly parents. For these individuals, hiring a domestic worker/babysitter/carer for the elderly is a way to pursue new models of parenthood and family life that do not of necessity entail a long, daily, physical commitment towards their family members. One may speak of the search for a 'modern' version of domesticity that combines responsibilities towards loved ones with paid work and a professional career, inevitably reducing the amount of time spent as the *materfamilias* in the home.

The second category of employers includes those who have to delegate the actual performance of care and domestic work to paid workers, but who would probably prefer to do the work themselves. Lack of time and energy, distance from their children or parents, and commitments to other family members are usually the reasons why these employers cannot directly take charge of the care of their relatives or even clean their own apartments. Thus employing someone is a second-best option, but it comes at the cost of feelings of guilt or betrayal. This type of employer expresses discomfort in the employment relationship. In so doing, they put forward traditional views on commitment towards their households which is ultimately detrimental to the relationships with the women to whom they delegate parts of their mothering and care duties.

2.5   Differences Between Countries

Today, how the commodification of care for elderly people, sick people and young children is organized – and in some cases supported – by public measures, differs from country to country. In fact, authors speak of conflicting tendencies within the political economy of care depending on the context (Esping-Andersen, 1999; Mahon & Robinson, 2011). In the past, there was a more distinct range, from systems that traditionally relied on non-paid care from family members (particularly women), to countries where such assistance was, partially at least, in the hands of the state. They range from the informal hiring of a migrant domestic worker (live-in or live-out) in the home, as is common in Italy, Spain or Greece; to the hiring through formal care schemes managed by private agencies authorized by the state, as often happens in the UK; to receiving services directly organized by state agencies, as is the case predominantly in Sweden or the Netherlands. One may also notice that the latest trends in the field of care provision for children, elderly and/or disabled people in Western Europe are increasingly following in the footsteps of the Australian and North American examples, in opening to for-profit care providers of various sizes and their adoption of profit-oriented business models in the management of service provision and human resources (Farris & Marchetti, 2017).

Another important context-dependent factor concerns the 'culture of care', which differs from country to country (and sometimes even within the same country). Indeed, as Francesca Degiuli (2010) emphasizes, the decision by care receivers to turn to private employment in home-based care cannot simply be explained by the greater or lesser availability of services and structures. It is rather based on shared cultural values and care traditions. For example, Pei Chia Lan (2018) notes that in the Asian context, the persistence of cultural norms that care for ageing parents will be provided 'in-house' by female family members is a notable impediment to the outsourcing of care.

The different modality of these arrangements can be tackled by the metaphor of the 'care diamond', which Kofman and Raghuram (2015) first introduced to explain how different actors, each placed at a corner of this diamond figure, contributed to shape the actual form of care provision. These actors were identified in the household of the care receiver, the state through welfare provision, and the not-for-profit sector, which through religious or other local voluntary organizations used to provide assistance to needy individuals. These actors were seen as distinct and mutually exclusive. However, this separation now seems to have faded away, especially since states are increasingly in favour of involving more actors.

This perspective helps us to understand the relationship between the welfare state and the 'refamiliarization' of those care commitments in the 1980s and 1990s that in some countries had previously been taken up by the state. This refamiliarization has not led to the re-establishment of previous systems of unpaid care provision, rather it has created a massive demand for privatized services because families have not (or not fully) returned to the traditional care model. They have started to outsource at least part of their care commitments (Ungerson, 1997). As Pavolini and

Ranci (2008) later observed, during these decades there has been 'a progressive decrease in the ability of family networks to provide support owing to the increase in the old age dependency ratio and the female activity rate' (p. 246). The combination of these processes of privatization and refamiliarization did unsettle the borders between the different European welfare regimes, according to Esping-Andersen (1996).

In other terms, households today are using their own family budget in order to purchase market-based services that had previously been provided by public nurseries, rest homes and hospitals, or that had been performed by members of the household itself (usually women). The problem is that when assessing the care which is needed and the resources available to acquire it, these households are often torn between the demands of the family and the functioning of the care market. For this reason, as mentioned before, it is important to think of employers as also caregivers, at least for the tasks which – for different reasons – are not delegated to a paid carer.

An overview of some care settings around the world will show that in countries like Italy, France and Belgium, there is a strong intervention by the state in supporting employers to individually 'buy' care service through allowances for families with disabled and seriously ill members, or young children. In Italy, this has been seen as an incentive for the emergence of what has been called a 'migrant-in-the-family' model whereby families become direct employers of migrant care workers (Ambrosini, 2013; Degiuli, 2010).

In Germany, the state intervenes in supporting the functioning of the market by emphasizing the role of employment agencies and other intermediaries specialized in this sector. In the UK, there is a divided market: since affluent families receive no allowances, they resort to private agencies from which they hire care workers, while working-class families who are recipients of cash benefits payments use it to cover general family expenses and only to a smaller extent to employ a private caregiver (Van Hooren, 2012).

Outside Europe, scenarios vary. In East Asia, countries like South Korea and Japan have a long-standing tradition of an institutional approach to care services and are reluctant to incorporate foreigners in their workforce on nationalistic grounds (Lan, 2018; Peng, 2017). Hong-Kong and Singapore, by contrast, have very personalized conceptions of care provision, with high levels of employment of foreigners within a liberal market approach (Peng, 2018), similar to the European migrant-in-the-family model. Halfway between these approaches is Taiwan, which has a tradition of public provision of healthcare and elder care, and yet when it comes to care for the elderly and disabled mainly relies on a liberalized system of intermediary agencies to employ migrant workers (Cheng, 2003; Lan, 2007).

Something different happens in the two countries that are considered the largest employers of domestic workers, Brazil and India, with a tradition of service work provided by girls (and some men), internal migrants, or ethnicized groups. This also happens in other places such as Ecuador, Bolivia and the Caribbean (Herrera, 2016; Martelotte, 2016; Masi de Casanova, 2013), south and central African countries (Ally, 2009), China, and South Asia (Neetha, 2018; Peng, 2017). Here domestic workers often live together with employers' families for many years, to satisfy their care needs as they change through various life stages: from taking care of children, to caring for the elderly.

A different model is in place when a foreign worker is employed for a limited number of years, with the explicit function of taking care of children before they grow up, or of elderly relatives in the final years of their life. This model is the same in very different places, from Canada and the US (Michel & Peng, 2017; Romero, 2018), to Lebanon, Israel and Middle Eastern countries (Fernandez et al., 2014; Liebelt, 2011; Ozyegin, 2010), to countries in the European Union. The implications of this model in its interconnection with international migration policies will be explored below, in relation to the question of the home as a site of governance of migration (Box 2.2).

Box 2.2: The Corporatization of Care in the United Kingdom, Sweden and Italy

The transformations in welfare and care provision in industrialized countries with large, ageing populations can be seen in the light of what we call the corporatization of care (Farris & Marchetti, 2017). Looking at the the examples of the United Kingdom, Sweden and Italy, we see how this process has taken place in countries associated with very different welfare models, care regimes and political traditions, which have been labelled respectively *liberal*, *social democratic* and *familistic* (Esping-Andersen, 1996).

The main differences between them can be summarized as follows:

- The United Kingdom: the elder care and childcare sectors are dominated by for-profit actors.
- Sweden: corporatized care is almost exclusively confined to the elder care sector, while the childcare sector is still mostly run by the state, or outsourced to not-for-profit actors.
- Italy: the presence of for-profit companies in the care sector is traditionally very limited, both in the case of elder care and childcare, where the not-for-profit sector or commodified forms of home-based care prevail.

Despite these differences, in all three countries the number of for-profit care providers has grown at a dramatic pace over the last decade. Even though the presence of for-profit companies is still very limited in Italy, or is confined to the elder care sector in Sweden, their exceptional expansion into the space in just a few years speaks of significant developments in investment in the care sector.

2.6   The Role of States

We may say that generally, the role of states in this realm is highly problematic. Increasingly since the 1990s, states have encouraged the marketization of care by relegating its provision to the private care providers and relying on competition among them. During the same period, as Tseng and Wang (2013) argue, states have been able to progressively delegate to employers (that is, care receivers) a series of important commitments and responsibilities which are vital to the functioning of the system. In Clare Ungerson's (1997) view, the 1980s and 1990s mark the crisis of welfare and the consequent refamiliarization of those care commitments that had previously been fulfilled by the state. This refamiliarization has created a demand for privatized services, since families are no longer able (or willing) to satisfy all the care needs of their households to the extent that they were in the past, and have therefore started to outsource at least part of their care commitments.

In Europe, care is probably the welfare sector that has been most privatized by state reforms in contrast with health, education, pensions and so forth (Daly, 2012; Ferrera, 2005; Graziano et al., 2011). The way European states are doing this varies greatly from country to country, with different policy approaches in place (see Picchi, 2016). In fact, since the 1990s, several Western European countries have reformed their long-term care system and promoted home-based care as a way to save on social care costs. In some countries there is a strong intervention by the state in supporting employers to buy the service by means of the monetization of allowances for households with disabled and seriously ill members, or for households with young children. In other cases, the state intervenes in supporting the functioning of the market by emphasizing the role of agencies, as we will discuss more in detail in Sect. 3.6. Thus we see how the role of states is central to making some market actors more influential. Governments are those who 'authorize, support or enforce the introduction of markets, the creation of relationships between buyers and sellers and the use of market mechanisms to allocate care' (Brennan et al., 2012, 379).

In other words, states have withdrawn from being direct providers of care, but they still retain other functions which greatly influence this sector. First of all, states have an important regulatory function, which explains why 'the commodification of care has gone hand in hand with an increase in public coverage and public regulation' (Pavolini & Ranci, 2008, p. 247). States are providing the normative framework and work regulations that allow private companies or individuals to offer their services within the households (Da Roit, 2019; Estévez-Abe & Hobson, 2015; Shire, 2015).

It is also worth noting, as Pavolini et al. (2012) point out, that these transformations in the role and function of state in care provision occurred in parallel to a reorganization of the 'level' at which decisions concerning these issues are taken. In countries like Italy, a progressive decentralization of state functions has had important repercussions on social services, health, education and welfare generally (Ferrera, 2005). Local public authorities such as regions and even municipalities, today have full powers in these realms. They are in charge of finding affordable, feasible and yet innovative solutions for the provision of services such as personal care for elderly and disabled people, despite the cutting of funds which limit direct public intervention in this field. In this scenario, local not-for-profit organizations such as cooperatives and associations become important allies by offering – at low cost– the means and structures to pursue new social policies.

There are a number of mechanisms through which the state can frame the emergence and functioning of a private care market. In Triandafyllidou and Marchetti (2015), we provide an overview of such mechanisms for several European countries. In the first place, states may introduce intermediaries in working relationships, such as employment agencies. An example of this is the voucher system which was introduced in Belgium in 2004, a policy of housework vouchers (*titres-services*) which allows households to officially purchase weekly housework services from an authorized agency (Camargo, 2015). Secondly, states can enforce specific occupational measures to promote (and influence) the private employment of domestic and care workers. Particularly relevant is the case when states take advantage of the growth of care market-services to channel unemployed local women into this work sector (Humer & Hrženjak, 2015; Van Walsum, 2011). Finally, states strongly intervene in the care market with explicit policies for the recruitment of migrants. I will come back to this in the following chapter of this book. For now, we can briefly mention au pair employment schemes (Cox & Busch, 2018; Kristensen, 2015; Pelechova, 2015), amnesty for undocumented migrants employed in this sector, and the establishment of bilateral agreements with countries of origin for recruitment in this field. The composition of the labour force will have a different character depending on existing bilateral agreements, including pre-departure training programmes and quota-based policies concerning workers' countries of origin (Kofman & Raghuram, 2015). Thus, states are important actors in dictating the rules and conditions of migrant workers' recruitment, which is of paramount importance today, given the high percentage of international migrants employed in all forms of care provision.

On the intertwining of state policies on welfare and migration, and the corresponding care market, Franca Van Hooren (2012) has offered the following three examples from Europe. She argues that different welfare systems lead to different types of migration, care arrangements and specific 'care markets'. First of all, she highlights the Italian 'familialistic care regime', which provides cash allowances to families, giving incentives for the emergence of a 'transnational market familialism' (Näre, 2013) or the migrant-in-the-family system (Bettio et al., 2006) whereby families become employers of migrant care workers. Secondly, we have the British care regime, where care is increasingly transformed into cash payments, with strong inequalities affecting the resulting care service market. More families receive no payments and hence resort to a private agency care market from which they hire care workers. At the same time, those families that are recipients of the Attendance Allowance (AA) in cash use it to cover peripheral costs like transport, food and fuel, while they rely on adult family members, friends and only to a smaller extent on professional care services for the actual care work. The third and last example is the

Dutch welfare system, which relies on the provision of care services that are publicly financed. Thus individuals rely on the public system for personal care, or on family members. There is no market for privately purchased personal care services and thus the demand for migrant care workers is very low (Van Hooren, 2012, p. 142).

Barbara Da Roit and Bernard Weicht (2013) find that Germany, Austria, Italy and Spain rely mainly on migrant care workers employed in the household, while the Netherlands, Norway, Sweden and the UK tend to rely more on the formal sector and on services provided by public organizations or private companies. Thus, they partly confirm the distinction introduced by Van Hooren (2012) between familialistic care regimes leading to migrant-in-the-family care models, and liberal regimes leading to migrant-in-the-market models. They indeed show that the migrant-in-the-family model adopted in Austria and Germany is the result of limited publicly available services, cash-for-care programmes, and the segregation of migrants in low-skilled jobs (Da Roit & Weicht, 2013, p. 479).

Da Roit and Weicht find that the segregated labour market and the presence of undocumented migrants willing to work as domestic workers are sufficient factors leading to a migrant-in-the-family model even in the absence of generous cash-for-care benefits (for example in Italy and Spain). At the same time, they find that while the absence of uncontrolled cash benefits and of a large informal economy are strong predictors of a migrant-in-formal-care model as occurs in the Netherlands, France, Sweden and Norway, they are not sufficient conditions. For example, the UK satisfies these conditions but is characterized by a strong presence of the private sector and formal care arrangements through private providers. It is probably a combination of the public expenditure on formal care services with the absence of uncontrolled cash-for-care programmes and the absence of an informal economy of care that leads to the specific national care model. Different 'care packages' are available depending on the context, and employers choose between various combinations of care services (Da Roit, 2010).

Another example of the overlap between state and markets in care provision is what we can call bureaucratized care, organized in a very different way from that based on private employment by individual households. Today this tendency is common in northern European countries such as Denmark (Cancedda, 2011), the Netherlands, Sweden, Norway (Da Roit & Weicht, 2013) and the UK (Shutes & Chiatti, 2012). Whether it is in a company or in the non-profit sector, bureaucratized care work is characterized by the intermediary role of care providers who act as employers of the care workers; they are responsible for recruiting, managing and organizing the work. Bureaucratized care work usually involves a collective dimension (that is, the organization of workers in teams) and some monitoring and tutoring provided by managers. In contrast to the one-to-one relationship between employer and employee in traditional home-based care, these care workers can be assigned to any of the care provider's clients. Finally, domestic chores tend to be organized on the basis of industrial criteria, as a certain amount of time is allocated for each task and each service provision is planned with cost-efficiency in mind.

Such emphasis on bureaucratized and industry-like forms of home care provision indicates that it is necessary to investigate the interaction between the multiplicity of actors that today intervenes in the realm of the commodification of care, such as private companies, not-for-profit cooperatives, public authorities, and so forth, and thus to broaden the perspective beyond the family as the realm of care (Kofman & Raghuram, 2009; Näre & Nordberg, 2016; Williams, 2010; Yeates, 2009). In a wider perspective, and following Clare Ungerson (1997), it is also important to look at these developments from the perspective of gender, race and class differences.

Responding to these debates, in Marchetti and Scrinzi (2014) we focused on migrant workers in bureaucratized settings, namely not-for-profit social cooperatives that provide home-based care services for the elderly in Italy. We documented both the application of bureaucratized and industry-like logics to the daily administration of not-for-profit care providers, and how the racialized and gendered profiling of workers plays a role in this type of organization. Indeed, it is important to draw attention to how, in bureaucratized care provision in Europe, the racialization and feminization of these jobs continues to shape the conditions for the large-scale employment therein of women with migrant backgrounds.

References

Ally, S. A. (2009). *From servants to workers: South African domestic workers and the democratic state*. Cornell University Press.

Ambrosini, M. (2013). *Irregular migration and invisible welfare*. Palgrave Macmillan.

Andall, J. (2000). *Gender, migration and domestic service: The politics of black women in Italy*. Ashgate.

Anderson, B. (2000). *Doing the dirty work? The global politics of domestic labor*. Zed Books.

Anthias, F., & Yuval-Davis, N. (1992). *Racialized boundaries: Race, nation, gender, colour and the anti-racist struggle*. Routledge.

Anttonen, A., & Haïkiö, L. (2011). Care 'going market': Finnish elderly-care policies in transition. *Nordic Journal of Social Research, 2*, 1–21.

Arango Gaviria, L. G. (1997). 'La clase obrera tiene dos sexos': Avances de los estudios latinoamericanos sobre género y trabajo. *Nómadas, 6*, 1–13.

Baumol, W. J. (1967). Macroeconomics of unbalanced growth: The anatomy of urban crisis. *American Economic Review, 57*(3), 415–426.

Bettio, F., Simonazzi, A., & Villa, P. (2006). Change in care regimes and female migration: The 'care drain' in the Mediterranean. *Journal of European Social Policy, 16*(3), 271–285.

Blunt, A., & Dowlings, R. (2006). *Home*. Routledge.

Brennan, D., Cass, B., Himmelweit, S., & Szebehely, M. (2012). The marketisation of care: Rationales and consequences in Nordic and liberal care regimes. *Journal of European Social Policy, 22*(4), 377–391.

Camargo, B. (2015). Outsourcing housework: Clients, agencies and the voucher system in Brussels. In A. Triandafyllidou & S. Marchetti (Eds.), *Employers, agencies and immigration: Care work in Europe*. Ashgate.

Cancedda, A. (2011). *Employment in household services*. European Foundation for the Improvement of Living and Working Conditions.

Cheng, S. J. A. (2003). Rethinking the globalization of domestic service: Foreign domestics, state control, and the politics of identity in Taiwan. *Gender & Society, 17*(2), 166–186.

Clarke, J. (2006). Consumers, clients or citizens? Politics, policy and practice in the reform of social care. *European Societies, 8*(3), 423–442.

Connell, J. (2008). *The Global Health care chain: From the Pacific to the world*. Routledge.

Cox, R., & Busch, N. (2018). *As an equal? Au pairing in the twenty-first century*. Zed Books.

Cranford, C. J., & Miller, D. (2013). Emotion management from the Client's perspective: The case of personal home care. *Work, Employment & Society, 27*(5), 785–801.

Da Roit, B. (2010). *Strategies of care: Changing elderly Care in Italy and the Netherlands*. Amsterdam University Press.

Da Roit, B., & Moreno-Fuentes, F. J. (2019). Cash for care and care employment:(missing) debates and realities. *Social Policy & Administration, 53*(4), 596–611.

Da Roit, B., & Weicht, B. (2013). Migrant care work and care, migration and employment regimes: A fuzzy-set analysis. *Journal of European Social Policy, 23*(5), 469–486.

Daly, M. (2012). Making policy for care: Experience in Europe and its implications in Asia. *International Journal of Sociology and Social Policy, 32*(11/12), 2–20.

Davidoff, L. (2003). Gender and the 'great divide': Public and private in British gender history. *Journal of Women's History, 15*(1), 11–26.

Degiuli, F. (2010). The burden of long-term care: How Italian family care-givers become employers. *Ageing and Society, 30*(5), 755–777.

De Regt, M. (2009). Preferences and prejudices: Employers views on domestic workers in the Republic of Yemen. *Signs, 34*(3), 559–581.

Eaton, S. C. (1996). *Beyond unloving care: Promoting innovation in elder care through public policy*. Radcliffe Public Policy Institute, Changing Work in America Series.

Esping-Andersen, G. (Ed.). (1996). *Welfare states in transition: Social security in the new global economy*. Sage.

Esping-Andersen, G. (1999). *Social foundations of post-industrial economies*. Oxford University Press.

Estévez-Abe, M., & Hobson, B. (2015). Outsourcing domestic (care) work: The politics, policies, and political economy. *Social Politics: International Studies in Gender, State & Society, 22*(2), 133–146.

Farris, S. R., & Marchetti, S. (2017). From the commodification to the corporatization of care: European perspectives and debates. *Social Politics, 24*(2), 109–131.

Fernandez, B., De Regt, M., & Currie, G. (Eds.). (2014). *Migrant domestic workers in the Middle East: The home and the world*. Springer.

Ferrera, M. (2005). *The boundaries of welfare: European integration and the new spatial politics of social protection*. University Press.

Folbre, N. (2012). *For love and money*. Sage.

Fonseca, C., & Brites, J. (2014). Cuidados profesionales en el espacio doméstico: algunas reflexiones desde Brasil. Diálogo entre Jurema Brites y Claudia Fonseca. *Íconos: Revista de Ciencias Sociales, 50*, 163–174.

Gallo, E., & Scrinzi, F. (2016). *Migration, masculinities and reproductive labour: Men of the home*. Springer.

Galvaan, R., Peters, L., Smith, T., Brittain, M., Menegaldo, A., Rautenbach, N., & Wilson-Poe, A. (2015). Employers' experiences of having a live-in domestic worker: Insights into the relationship between privilege and occupational justice. *South African Journal of Occupational Therapy., 45*(1), 41–46.

Glendinning, C. (2008). Increasing choice and control for older and disabled people: A critical review of new developments in England. *Social Policy & Administration, 42*(5), 451–469.

Graziano, P. R., Jaquot, S., & Palier, B. (Eds.). (2011). *The EU and the domestic politics of welfare state reforms: Europa, Europae*. Palgrave Macmillan.

Guillaumin, C. (1997). *La confrontation des féministes en particulier au racisme en général. Remarques sur les relations du féminisme à ses sociétés*. Paper presented at the Journée de l'ANEF, Les féministes face à l'antisémitisme et au racisme, Paris.

Gutiérrez-Rodríguez, E. (2010). *Migration, domestic work and affect: A Decolonial approach on value and the feminization of labor.* Routledge.

Herrera, G. (2016). *Trabajo doméstico, cuidados y familias transnacionales en América Latina: reflexiones sobre un campo en construcción* (p. 31). Les Cahiers ALHIM. Les Cahiers ALHIM.

Hochschild, A. (2012). *The outsourced self: Intimate life in market times.* Henry Holt and Company.

Humer, Ž., & Hrženjak, M. (2015). When the state steps in: An experiment of subsidised hiring of domestic workers in Slovenia. In A. Triandafyllidou & S. Marchetti (Eds.), *Employers, agencies and immigration: Care work in Europe.* Ashgate.

Kingma, M. (2007). Nurses on the move: A global overview. *Health Services Research, 42,* 1281–1298.

Kofman, E. (2012). Gendered labour migrations in Europe and emblematic migratory figures. *Journal of Ethnic and Migration Studies, 39*(4), 579–600.

Kofman, E., & Raghuram, P. (2009). *The implications of migration for gender and care regimes in the south* (Social policy and development programme 8). United nations research institute for social Development.

Kofman, E., & Raghuram, P. (2015). *Gendered migrations and global social reproduction.* Palgrave Macmillan.

Kristensen, G. K. (2015). A fair deal? Paid domestic labour in social democratic Norway. In A. Triandafyllidou & S. Marchetti (Eds.), *Employers, agencies and immigration: Care work in Europe.* Ashgate.

Kristensen, G. K. (2017). My home is my castle. The Norwegian home in times of paid migrant domestic labour. *Culture and Organization, 23*(4), 277–290.

Lan, P. C. (2007). *Legal servitude and free illegality: Migrant 'guest' workers in Taiwan. Asian Diasporas: New Formations, New Conceptions* (pp. 253–277).

Lan, P. C. (2018). Bridging ethnic differences for cultural intimacy: Production of migrant care workers in Japan. *Critical Sociology, 44*(7–8), 1029–1043.

Liebelt, C. (2011). *Caring for the 'Holy Land': Filipina domestic Workers in Israel.* Berghahn Books.

Lundström, C. (2013). "Mistresses" and "maids" in transnational "contact zones": Expatriate wives and the intersection of difference and intimacy in Swedish domestic spaces in Singapore. *Women's Studies International Forum, 36,* 44–53.

Lutz, H. (2008). *Migration and domestic work: A European perspective on a global theme.* Ashgate.

Mahon, R., & Robinson, F. (2011). *Feminist ethics and social policy: Towards a new global political economy of care.* UBC Press.

Marchetti, S. (2015). 'Mum seems happy': Relatives of dependent elders and the difficult task to employ a migrant care-giver. In A. Triandafyllidou & S. Marchetti (Eds.), *Employers, agencies and immigration: Paying for care* (pp. 93–109). Ashgate.

Marchetti, S., & Scrinzi, F. (2014). *Gendered and racialised constructions of work in bureaucratised care services in Italy.* Robert Schuman Centre for Advanced Studies Research Paper (2014/123).

Martelotte, L. (2016). El cuidado en América Latina. Aprendizajes y desafíos pendientes. *Debate Feminista, 49,* 321–326.

Masi de Casanova, E. (2013). Embodied inequality: The experience of domestic work in urban Ecuador. *Gender & Society, 27*(4), 561–585.

Massey, D. (1994). *Space, place and gender.* Polity Press.

Mérola, G. (1985). Feminismo: Un movimiento social. *Nueva Sociedad, 78,* 112–117.

Michel, S., & Peng, I. (2017). *Gender, migration, and the work of care: A multi-scalar approach to the Pacific rim.* Springer.

Molinier, P., & Arango, L. G. (2014). *El trabajo y la ética del cuidado.* Universidad Nacional de Colombia/La Carreta editores.

Momsen, J. (1999). Maids on the move. In J. Momsen (Ed.), *Gender, migration and domestic service* (pp. 1–21). Routledge.

Näre, L. (2013). The ethics of transnational market familism: Inequalities and hierarchies in the Italian elderly care. *Ethics and Social Welfare, 7*(2), 184–197.

Näre, L., & Nordberg, C. (2016). Neoliberal postcolonialism in the media: Constructing Filipino nurse subjects in Finland. *European Journal of Cultural Studies, 19*, 16–32.

Needham, C. (2011). *Personalising public services: Understanding the personalisation narrative.* Policy Press.

Neetha, N. (2018). *Working at others' homes: The specifics and challenges of paid domestic work.* Tulika Books.

Ozyegin, G. (2010). *Untidy gender: Domestic Service in Turkey.* Temple University Press.

Parreñas, R. S., & Boris, E. (Eds.). (2010). *Intimate labors: Cultures, technologies and the politics of care.* University Press.

Pavolini, E., & Ranci, C. (2008). Restructuring the welfare state: Reforms in long-term care in western European countries. *Journal of European Social Policy, 18*(3), 246–259.

Pavolini, E., Colombo, S., & Neri, S. (2012). *Il Giano bi-fronte: la diffusione di forme di welfare contrattuale in Italia.* Espanet Italia.

Pelechova, L. (2015). Au pairs and changing family needs in the United Kingdom. In A. Triandafyllidou & S. Marchetti (Eds.), *Employers, agencies and immigration: Care work in Europe.* Ashgate.

Peng, I. (2017). Explaining exceptionality: Care and migration policies in Japan and South Korea. In S. Michel & I. Peng (Eds.), *Gender, migration, and the work of care: A multi-scalar approach to the Pacific rim.* Springer International Publishing.

Peng, I. (2018). Shaping and reshaping care and migration in east and Southeast Asia. *Current Sociology, 44*(7–8), 1117–1132.

Picchi, S. (2016). The elderly care and domestic services sector during the recent economic crisis: The case of Italy, Spain and France. *Investigaciones feministas: papeles de estudios de mujeres, feministas y de género, 1*(7), 169.

Poo, A. J., & Conrad, A. (2009). *The age of dignity: Preparing for the elder boom in a changing America.* The New Press.

Quiroga Diaz, N. (2009). Economías feminista, social y solidaria. Respuestas heterodoxas a la crisis de reproducción en América Latina. *Íconos: Revista de Ciencias Sociales, 33*, 77–89.

Radziwinowiczówna, A., Rosińska-Kordasiewicz, A., & Kloc-Nowak, W. (2018). *Ethnomorality of care: Migrants and their aging parents.* Routledge.

Romero, M. (2018). Reflections on globalized care chains and migrant women workers. *Critical Sociology, 44*(7–8), 1179–1189.

Shire, K. (2015). Family supports and insecure work: The politics of household service employment in conservative welfare regimes. *Social Politics, 22*(2), 193–219.

Shutes, I., & Chiatti, C. (2012). Migrant labour and the marketization of care for older people: The employment of migrant care workers by families and service providers. *Journal of European Social Policy, 22*(4), 392–405.

Shutes, I., & Walsh, K. (2012). Negotiating user preferences, discrimination, and demand for migrant labour in long-term care. *Social Politics: International Studies in Gender, State & Society, 19*(1), 78–104.

Simonazzi, A. (2011). Home care and cash transfers: The search for a sustainable elderly care model. In E. Addis, P. de Villota, F. Degavre, & J. Eriksen (Eds.), *Gender and wellbeing: Interactions between work, family and public policies* (pp. 127–145). Ashgate.

Stevens, M., Glendinning, C., Jacobs, S., Moran, N., Challis, D., Manthorpe, J., Fernandez, J.-L., Jones, K., Knapp, M., & Netten, A. (2011). Assessing the role of increasing choice in English social care services. *Journal of Social Policy, 40*(2), 257–274.

Triandafyllidou, A., & Marchetti, S. (Eds.). (2015). *Employers, agencies and immigration: Care work in Europe.* Ashgate.

Tseng, Y., & Wang, H. (2013). Governing migrant workers at a distance: Managing the temporary status of guestworkers in Taiwan. *International Migration, 51*(4), 1–19.

Ungerson, C. (1997). Social politics and the commodification of care. *Social Politics, International Studies in Gender, State & Society, 4*(3), 362–381.

Van Hooren, F. (2012). Varieties of migrant care work: Comparing patterns of migrant labour in social care. *Journal of European Social Policy, 22*(2), 133–147.

Van Walsum, S. (2011). Regulating migrant domestic work in the Netherlands: Opportunities and pitfalls. *Canadian Journal of Women and the Law/Revue Femmes et Droit, 23*, 141–165.

Vega, C. (2009). *Culturas del cuidado en transición: Espacios, sujetos e imaginarios en una sociedad de migración.* Editorial UOC.

Vega, C., & Gutiérrez Rodríguez, E. (2014). Nuevas aproximaciones a la organización social del cuidado: debates latinoamericanos. Presentación del dossier. *Íconos: Revista de Ciencias Sociales, 50*, 9–26.

Williams, F. (2010). Migration and care: Themes, concepts and challenges. *Social Policy and Society, 9*(3 July), 385–396.

Williams, F. (2011). Towards a transnational analysis of the political economy of care. In R. Mahon & F. Robinson (Eds.), *Feminist ethics and social policy: Towards a new global political economy of care.* UBC Press.

Wolkowitz, C. (2006). *Bodies at work.* Sage.

Yeates, N. (2004). Global care chains. *International Feminist Journal of Politics, 6*, 369–391.

Yeates, N. (2009). *Globalizing care economies and migrant workers: Explorations in global care chains.* Palgrave Macmillan.

Yeatman, A. (2009). Theoretical perspectives on individualization and the delivery of welfare services. In A. In Yeatman, G. W. Dowsett, M. Fine, & D. Gursansky (Eds.), *Individualization and the delivery of welfare services: Contestation and complexity* (pp. 1–116). Palgrave Macmillan.

Yeoh, B., & Huang, S. (1999). Singapore women and foreign domestic workers: Negotiating domestic work and motherhood. In J. Momsen (Ed.), *Gender, migration and domestic service* (pp. 273–296). Routledge.

Yuval-Davis, N., Wemyss, G., & Cassidy, K. (2019). *Bordering.* Wiley.

Zelizer, V. (2009). *The purchase of intimacy.* University Press.

Chapter 3
Migration

3.1 Domestic Workers and Migration Policies

State policies may strongly influence the employment of migrants for care and domestic work (Ruhs & Anderson, 2010). Both sending and receiving countries have adopted mechanisms to channel migrants (especially women) into this specific occupation. The care market-oriented scenario described in the previous pages creates a growing demand for a (female) migrant labour force employed to work for longer hours and at lower wages than local workers (Anderson & Shutes, 2014; Cangiano & Shutes, 2010). These migrant care workers are generally disadvantaged by policies privileging skilled over unskilled migration, as well as by legislation denying (long-term) residence permits to people employed in the care sector. Policies that make the regular employment of migrants very difficult contribute to the under-valuation of these jobs, which are generally assigned to the most vulnerable and stigmatized subjects in each national context (Lan, 2006). Women migrating to work in the domestic and private care sector face a complex landscape of migration and labour regulations that is extremely difficult to navigate. The situation is also problematic for households that cannot find appropriate or affordable care within declining welfare states and among fellow nationals reluctant to take these jobs, but are forbidden or discouraged from directly hiring a domestic worker who is a third-country national. As a consequence, irregular migration and informal work are expanding within the realm of private homes.

We have already seen that the composition of the labour force in each country also depends on the features of bilateral agreements between countries of origin and destination. Among those open to migrants in domestic and care work, we find countries that set quotas for the number of migrants accepted from specific nationalities and specific occupations. In Italy, for example, there is a specific quota for domestic and care workers. Also, migrant domestic workers may or may not be part of regularization procedures for undocumented migrants. Other countries strongly contrast with this tendency. They are reluctant to welcome foreigners in this sector

© The Author(s) 2022
S. Marchetti, *Migration and Domestic Work*, IMISCOE Research Series,
https://doi.org/10.1007/978-3-031-11466-3_3

and it is therefore almost impossible to receive a residence permit if you are a migrant doing domestic and care work (Triandafyllidou, 2013). In some of these countries, however, the demand for full-time paid domestic work has been channelled into au pair schemes, which are increasingly popular among families with young children that do not have other resources for the employment of foreign workers (see Cox, 2007; Isaksen, 2010).

In relation to these different settings, it is important to question how gender, race and migration play a role in the management and organization of the workforce in these services, and in paid domestic and care work more generally. Migrant women are disadvantaged by policies privileging skilled migration as well as by legislation denying work permits to those who have migrated to reunite with their families. At the same time, xenophobic discourses and gendered representations have developed in European societies, distinguishing between 'good' migrants and those whose integration is deemed impossible on the basis of ideas of the migrants' 'cultural proximity' or 'distance' (Spijkerboer & Van Walsum, 2007). The ways in which these racialized and gendered representations inform the organization of domestic and care labour have attracted considerable scholarly attention. Ethnographic studies of domestic service show that, due to the specific nature of care work, 'naturalization' – meaning the normalization of gendered and of racialized difference between people – serves to make the emotional labour and skills of migrant domestic workers invisible, on the basis of the idea of a 'cultural' predisposition for care among women of certain nationalities (Marchetti & Scrinzi, 2011; Scrinzi, 2013).

Less is known, on the other hand, about the role played by racism and ethnicity in the organization of work in what I called, in the previous chapter, bureaucratized care jobs. Black workers report experiences of racism from care recipients as well as from managers and co-workers (Timonen & Doyle, 2010). Care workers tend to enact ideas of cultural difference in their relationships with their co-workers, attributing positive qualities to their national group (Timonen & Doyle, 2010). Further, intermediaries between care recipients and caregivers, such as recruitment agencies, can play an important role in reproducing or challenging sexist and racializing ideas as well as the gendered and racialized division of work in the sector (Bakan & Stasiulis, 1994; Lendaro & Imdorf, 2012; Scrinzi, 2013) (Box 3.1).

3.2   Irregular Migration in Europe

The number of households employing a domestic worker is increasing across the European Union in response to the widespread privatization of the childcare and elder care sectors. Since public nurseries, homes for the elderly and hospitals can no longer satisfy their needs, European families have shifted to purchasing market-based care and cleaning services. Hiring a migrant domestic worker meets the demand for affordable yet high quality personal care, while offering a solution to native women who struggle to combine expectations about care commitments with

Box 3.1: Is Migration Good for Women?

Transposing Susan Moller Okin's (1999) famous question, 'Is multiculturalism good for women?', one could equally wonder 'Is migration good for women?'

On the one hand, the *positive* elements of migration for women can be summarized as follows:

- it presents an opportunity for women to escape oppressive marriages.
- women can gain economic independence by becoming self-sufficient.
- women can improve their social position in their community of origin thanks to remittances and donations.

For Parreñas (2001), such improvements could justify the decision to migrate even with the prospect of strong downgrading, in low-skilled and stigmatized jobs in the country of destination, as experienced by many migrants.

On the other hand, migration is seen as a source of vulnerability and danger in view of the following **negative** elements:

- the perilous journeys at the hands of smugglers.
- being exposed to the risk of sexual violence and unwanted pregnancies.
- the risk of being trafficked into slavery-like work in different labour sectors.
- the risk (for cleaners and carers) of isolation and abuse in employers' private homes.
- self-deprivation to satisfy commitments to financially support their communities in the country of origin.

For these reasons, migrant women and girls are considered to be at greater risk of physical and psychological suffering than men, especially when migration is for the purposes of an arranged marriage or when they flee their countries as refugees.

expectations from their workplace, and who would otherwise have to step out of the labour market.

Despite this expansion, in many EU countries it is still difficult, if at all possible, to legally hire a migrant domestic worker. An initial obstacle stems from the fact that the sector itself is often poorly regulated (see Table 3.1). Domestic workers lack specific legal protection in countries such as Greece, the UK, Denmark, Spain and the Netherlands. Poland does not actually recognize this work as proper work, relegating it to a 'personal service'. On the other hand, Italy, Austria, Belgium, France, Portugal and Sweden are positive examples of countries where the employment of domestic workers is regulated by a specific collective agreement. Table 3.1 summarizes the latest reports from the Bureau of Workers' Activities of the ILO (ACTRAV, 2013) and the European Union's Fundamental Rights Agency (FRA,

Table 3.1 Legal framework for the private employment of domestic workers

Country	Specific legislation for domestic work	Specific collective agreement	Application of collective agreements on agency recruitment	No specific law (application of general labour law)	Domestic work is *not* considered employment
Austria	x	x			
Belgium	x	x			
Denmark				x	
Finland	x				
France	x	x			
Germany		x			
Greece				x	
Hungary	x				
Ireland	x				
Italy	x	x			
Netherlands	x		x		
Poland					x
Portugal	x	x			
Spain	x		x		
Sweden		x			
UK				x	

Source: Compiled by the authors using data from ACTRAV/ILO and FRA, cit

2011) in order to show the variety of legal arrangements that frame the employment of domestic workers.

The second obstacle to the hiring of a migrant domestic worker comes from national policies on labour migration. Table 3.2 provides an overview of the migration policy frameworks that apply to migrant domestic workers. In countries like Denmark, Finland, the Netherlands and Germany, it is not possible for households to hire a foreigner in a legal way. In Belgium, France and Spain, by contrast, although this is possible in principle, it is made unfeasible in practice by a strict application of regulations against the employment of foreigners in low-skilled labour markets.

In countries like Italy and Greece, a quota system fixes the maximum number of people that can apply for a residence permit for employment as domestic workers or carers each year. However, these quotas are usually set on the basis of a regional estimate of demand for workers in this sector that does not reflect true demand. Indeed, household needs for care or cleaning tasks cannot be planned by families as employers-to-be in the same way that a private firm would do in the industrial or agricultural sectors. Care needs often arise unexpectedly (somebody falls ill, a child is born). So the whole system of annual quotas of labour demand in the domestic work sector is ill-equipped to respond to the needs of households.

Countries where hiring is possible may still have very different regulations concerning the recruitment system: in Italy, Belgium and the UK, the employer has to

Table 3.2 Legal framework for the employment of migrant domestic workers (Main countries)

Country	Possible to hire non-EU domestic workers	Market-test as barrier to hiring non-EU domestic workers	Quota limitations	Self-employment	Sponsor system	Au pairs as substitute channel
Austria	Yes			x		
Belgium	Yes	x		x	x	x
Denmark	No					x
Finland	No					x
France	Yes	x				
Germany	No					
Ireland	Yes					
Italy	Yes		x		x	
Netherlands	No					x
Poland	Yes					
Portugal	Yes					
Spain	Yes	x				
Sweden	Yes					x
UK	Yes				x	x
Hungary	Yes					
Greece	Yes		x			

Source: Compiled by Triandafyllidou and Marchetti (2014) using data from ACTRAV/ILO and FRA, cit

formally sponsor the trip and the stay of the worker, including financial support. Meanwhile in Austria, care workers are self-employed, which releases the households from any responsibility. Finally, it is also worth noting that in several countries where hiring a migrant for domestic work is not allowed, the au pair placement scheme has increasingly been abused by families as an opportunity to find affordable childcare and cleaning help, rather than as a cultural exchange experience for a young person as it is intended to be.

In many EU countries, legal migrant domestic work coexists with irregular stay and employment, with important repercussions on the fundamental rights of migrant domestic workers. A study by the Fundamental Rights Agency (FRA, 2011) and Anna Triandafyllidou (2013) on irregular migration in domestic work has shown how the specificities of domestic work (taking place inside the home, often with non-fixed hours and tasks) when intertwined with undocumented migration status and informal work arrangements can lead to particularly exploitative conditions of work and situations of extreme vulnerability.

The paid domestic work sector is exemplary of the labour market demand and supply dynamics in low-skilled sectors. Greece, Italy and Spain have met their demand in these sectors through repeated mass regularizations of undocumented migrants, many of whom, particularly women, are employed in care and cleaning jobs. Italy in particular implemented two large regularization programmes in 2002 and in 2009 especially targeting people in this sector. After the 2008 crisis, despite rising unemployment in these three countries that were in the eye of the Eurozone storm (with average unemployment at nearly 25 per cent in Greece and Spain in 2013 and 12 per cent and rising in Italy the same year), native women appeared reluctant to find employment in this sector. Even if the demand for cleaning and care services by middle class families – hit by recession and unemployment – had fallen, the domestic work sector was less influenced by the crisis than for instance, the construction industry, or agriculture (Bonifazi & Marini, 2013; Di Bartolomeo & Marchetti, 2016; Gonzalez-Enriquez, 2013; Maroukis, 2013).

In Triandafyllidou and Marchetti (2014), we argue that the EU needs a comprehensive, albeit differentiated, approach that takes into account the complexity of labour force supply and demand and the different economic cycles of individual member states. We also point to the need to acknowledge that there is a structural demand for a migrant labour force in certain occupations, which is related to long-term demographic processes such as the ageing of European societies; the configuration of nuclear families without extended support networks to cover the need to care for children, elderly or disabled people; and the participation of women in paid work outside the home. These processes are irreversible and persist even in periods of acute economic downturn.

In Triandafyllidou and Marchetti (2015) we proposed the creation of a proactive regulatory framework that would be adaptable to territorial and sectorial difference, but would also usefully provide a management framework for current and future flows in low-skill sectors. Such a sectorial approach could be successfully tested in the case of the wider domestic sector encompassing both cleaning and care work. This approach would complement the existing directives on training, research, students, intra-company transferees, highly skilled migrants and seasonal employment, listed above.

3.3   The Importance of Networks

It is in the light of the informality of the sector and the vulnerability of domestic workers that the question of networks is especially important. This is so at different levels. First, given the highly informal character of job recruitment in domestic and care work, networks play a great role in causing people to enter the sector, spreading information about new places of employment, types of work, and so on. The use of networks is also favoured by employers who prefer to hire women in a personal relationship with someone they already know and trust. Huw Vasey (2015) discusses the impact of networks on migrants' labour integration, saying that, in particular in the case of people in low-skilled occupations, the labour mobility of migrant workers is often not about skills per se, but about the opportunities that they find in each social context, due to dynamics within the host society but also within migrants' networks. Migrant domestic workers profit definitively from the support of their networks for their labour integration in the new country (Parreñas, 2001).

Following the seminal work of Pierrette Hondagneu-Sotelo (1994), social networks have been identified as an essential resource for domestic workers' empowerment. In their free time, when meeting with friends and colleagues outside the employers' houses, domestic workers can share contacts for better jobs, advice about mistreatment, and information about new legal and social services. They can learn about how to negotiate with employers concerning tasks and payment so that 'while the occupation remains largely unregulated by formal bureaucratic government agencies …, an intensive and informal social regulation is created by the domestic workers themselves' (Hondagneu-Sotelo, 1994, p. 61). In other words, social networks are a strategy for these workers to compensate for their exclusion from the formal labour market. However, social networks can also serve to 'divide' the market of migrant care and domestic work on unequal terms, creating internal boundaries and overshadowing people's autonomy in their labour mobility. For example, Anna Gavanas (2012) emphasizes how networks can increase the segmentation that characterizes this sector. This is especially so when domestic workers act as brokers for new job recruitments and they can thus favour their acquaintances in order to increase their prestige within the community – or they can provide jobs in exchange for economic compensation, which is particularly common among Eastern European domestic workers (Mazzacurati, 2005). This can also explain the competition between domestic workers from different national groups, as in the cases I will discuss in the following pages.

This tendency to competition often relates to the functioning of social network dynamics between migrants from different nationalities, the principles that organize them, and the impact of the economic crisis on them. Looking at the case of Georgian, Ukrainian and Polish women working in the Italian province of Reggio Emilia (Marchetti, 2017), the interconnections between these difference issues emerged at the following levels:

1. At the cultural and linguistic level: the research respondents felt connected at this level in the aftermath of socialist rule. This made it possible to share information and participate in the same social activities using their native languages (Polish, Ukrainian and Russian) which they could all understand a little. It also gave them a general sense of solidarity and commonality vis-à-vis their integration in Italy. At this level all three groups stood together with no major differentiations between Georgians, Poles and Ukrainians.
2. In relation to their migration trajectories in Italy: at this level, one could see the emulation of Polish migration patterns on the part of Ukrainians. This relationship built on previous historical cross-border connections between Ukraine and Poland which influenced Ukrainians' trajectories towards and within Italy. Georgians, by contrast, took a separate path.
3. Regarding free mobility and irregular migration: at this level, there was more similarity and interconnection between Georgians and Ukrainians, while Poles remaining separate. The need to obtain a residence permit to be in Italy placed Georgians and Ukrainians in similar conditions so that they tended to seek more long-term employment with regular contracts, often approaching local non-profit

services for support. Poles, conversely, tended to take more flexible and temporary jobs, since they could travel freely within the EU.

4. In relation to the impact of the economic crisis on the labour market of elder
   care: at this level the three groups entered into competition with each other. Their
   differences in legal status and economic need (depending on variations in the
   cost of living in their countries of origin) gave them different leverages to negotiate salaries and labour conditions with prospective employers. This upended the
   relationships between the groups, with Georgians having more opportunities to
   work than Poles, and Ukrainians in the middle. The crisis and the general impoverishment of employers' households had meant that the group that could sell
   itself the most cheaply for intensive labour had more opportunities to find work.

We see here the importance of looking at social network dynamics as processes
that go beyond nationality. On the one hand, this is so because some of the characteristics that are associated with particular national groups may also be found among
migrants from other national groups. This is demonstrated by the importance of the
socialist legacy, in cultural and linguistic terms, in shaping sentiments of solidarity
and support between women from different Eastern European countries. However,
the networks between national groups can function on the basis of interconnections
between some of these countries, but not all of them. On some issues, Poles and
Ukrainians are connected, while on some others the network is between Ukrainians
and Georgians. These contingent interconnections are explained, in my view, by
contextual factors: migration regulations, labour market dynamics, salaries, the cost
of living in the home country, the availability of specific knowledge, and so on. In
this perspective, the constitution and functioning of migrants' networks are not (or
not only) grounded on shared identities or cultural legacies, but more on contingent
external factors that push several groups to interact and support each other, though
they may be divided on other issues. The economic recession, in this sense, can be
seen as the external factor that breaks all possible supportive interactions between
the groups, increasing their competition, and inaugurating a dynamic in which
everyone is trying to take advantage of the market by exploiting the unique features
of their group (Box 3.2).

3.4   Care and Circular Migration

The European Commission's 'global approach to migration' promotes circular
migration as an 'efficient' way to manage labour migration within and from outside
the EU member states (see COM, 2007 and Council of Europe, 2009). In these
documents, workers' circular migration, meaning the going back and forth between
the country of origin and destination every few months, is portrayed as a profitable
tool to maximize the positive outcome of labour mobility in EU countries, while
reducing the possible negative impact of long-term migration, from the point of
view of the countries of settlement and of those of origin alike. When we examine
the case of circular migrant women in the Italian care sector, quite a different picture

Box 3.2: Migrants' Networks

Social networks are of great interest in migration studies to understand diasporas and transnationalism. In the classic definition by Douglas Massey, migrants' social networks are ties based on 'kinship, friendship, and shared community of origin', which can favourably influence an individual or household's decision to migrate (Massey et al., 1993, p. 448). The existence of networks represents a form of social capital for people who want to migrate: it provides them with possibilities of shelter and financial support upon arrival, directs them towards labour opportunities, and connects them to personal relationships and social activities with others belonging to the same community (Marin and Wellman 2011; Massey and Espinosa 1997). Networks are seen as something that 'reduces the costs and risks of movement', increasing the likelihood of migration. In some situations, social networks can determine the destination, and the social and economic activities in which migrants will engage after their arrival (Brezzi et al., 2010; Novotny and Hasman, 2015).

However, networks are not only a positive resource. They can represent an oppressive condition for many, in the form of ghettoization and isolation from other migrants and non-migrants, financial and material dependency on other group members, and the consolidation of hierarchies within a group. Network dynamics are not only based on unity and solidarity, but also reveal conflicts and divisions between members. As in the dynamic analyzed in this chapter, networks can convey knowledge sharing through the emulation of migratory paths, but they can also cause competition in the labour market and other spheres of migrants' social lives in host societies.

A crucial element in the making of social networks is the participation of members in specific economic activities. Networks can in fact be decisive in the formation of what are called 'ethnic labour niches', that is, when a single ethnic group occupies a predominant role in one employment sector or entrepreneurial activity. In the case of paid care givers and domestic workers, the same phenomenon can be observed in the early period of migrants' employment in the sector (Schrover et al., 2007).

---

appears. There one can find the practice of dividing a single job (i.e. caring for the same elderly person) between two or more women during the year, alternating for 2–3 months each. Interestingly, this 'job-sharing' is not portrayed by migrants as a limitation to their mobility. It is rather seen an *opportunity* that some migrants may opt for (cf. Mai, 2011). Entering this transnational form of 'job-sharing' emerges from an individual process of transformation, usually played out over several years. Becoming a circular migrant may be an important step in processes of migrants' subjectification, with a different meaning depending on their specific characteristics in terms of nationality, age and role in the household of origin. Circularity may be experienced in very different ways: its definition is stretched and adapted to each subject's needs and desires in relation to their work, and in the process, it may change its meaning.

Scholars have attempted to find a specific explanation for the fact that in some contexts more women than men engage in circular migration. Authors have referred to the unequal distribution of care commitments in the household of origin, which requires women to regularly go back home to accomplish their 'domestic obligations' more often than men (Ellis et al., 1996, p. 41). Cinzia Solari (2010) shows that in the context of Ukrainian migrant workers, the dominant gendered ideology favours the emigration of mature women rather than youngsters, and on a temporary basis rather than permanently, in order to preserve newly-formed young families and discourage the mass emigration of the new generation. As a consequence, mature mothers or grandmothers who otherwise have difficulty finding well-paid jobs in their home country, are the members of the household who can temporarily emigrate most profitably. Solari shows that the gender and age profile of the Ukrainians coming to Italy as home care workers is in line with a post-Soviet gendered ideology that prioritizes keeping young families together. The migratory decisions of mature Eastern European women are further determined by the negative transformations taking place – in Western as in Eastern countries – concerning the provision of welfare and the protection of social security rights for workers, children, sick and elderly people. We see that health and care services are increasingly being privatized across Europe with a strong emphasis on individual family strategies to find low-cost and yet high-quality solutions. Inequalities based on class and income thus become decisive for access to sanitary and medical care. Pension rights are seriously under threat, especially for those who have migrated or worked informally for some part of their career. At the same time, in Eastern Europe workers are induced to prolong their stay in the labour market in order to support both their children's access to an increasingly expensive education and costly medical care for ageing or sick relatives.

In fact, such circular East to West movements have thus far involved many Polish women going to Germany (Lutz, 2011; Morokvasic, 1994) and the Netherlands (Pool, 2003); as well as many Ukrainians going to Poland (Iglicka et al., 2011; Kindler, 2008) and Hungary (Caglar et al., 2011). In Italy one can also find circular migrants among Ukrainians, Poles, Georgians and other groups from the former Soviet bloc (Boccagni & Ambrosini, 2012; Marchetti & Venturini, 2014; Solari, 2010; Vianello, 2009; Vietti, 2010).

Circular migration in the home care sector typically consists of a rotation between two workers on a 3 or 4-month basis, and is portrayed in positive terms by many of the employers and workers I interviewed in the context of my 'Circular Care' research project. During this project, I found that circularity may also begin after years of steady work in the same place and labour sector. During this time, prospective circular carers build up the required social network among Italians and foreign colleagues and accumulate economic capital. This is in line with the argument made by Rhacel Parreñas for Filipinas in Japan, where she found that circularity is not to be understood only as a prelude to stable settlement (Parreñas, 2010). Moreover, my argument extended the conclusions of the Metoikos research project to the case of

Eastern European care workers. The Metoikos project on circular migration patterns in Southern and Central Eastern Europe observed that male migrants from Morocco and Albania start to rotate after several years of permanent emigration (Triandafyllidou, 2011); the same can be observed among Eastern European women care workers.

In 'Circular Care', I demonstrated that circularity in care work is not strongly characterized by unregulated employment and residency. Rather than misusing a tourist visa for labour purposes, the Ukrainian and Russian women I met start rotating only after having regularized their legal position and after having found regular employment. None of the Georgians that I interviewed was yet able to achieve a circular migration pattern, but several have it as a goal for the future. Poles, on the other hand, are generally working without a labour contract, but they are regular from the point of view of their residence status. I also showed that circular care cannot be equated with other forms of temporary work, especially seasonal work in agriculture. Unlike other sectors, it is important for these types of circular migrants to fulfil their tasks without interruption and without causing any distress to the care receiver. A reliable co-worker is thus essential to the performance of this job. For this reason, I argued, circular care can rather be seen as a transnational form of job sharing that has all the typical features of this employment modality in relation to the distribution of tasks, commitment towards the co-worker, and so on. Furthermore, circular migration in care work is not demand driven, nor is it produced by state programmes. On the contrary, it is actively sought out by workers who are causing this form of employment to spread in the sector. One could criticize this tendency by saying that they are contributing to the precarization of their own working conditions.

Going back to the Metoikos project, it is important to note that Ukrainian domestic and care workers circulating in Poland make use of tourist visas in order to enter and work irregularly. Iglicka et al., (2011) argue that in Poland this pattern usually precedes a more permanent migration. The cases I analyzed however were substantially different. I showed that women with regular working contracts sometimes decided to change to this form of employment after having worked permanently in Italy for several years. Moreover, they were not simply coming and going, but literally *organizing* a transnational rotation of workers. This tendency shows some novelty in comparison to informal and spontaneous types of circular migration, but also in comparison to more state-sponsored modalities, as in the case of mobility partnerships for the seasonal employment of Moroccan women in Spain's agriculture industry. In other words, while the circular migration of Ukrainians towards Poland could be framed as an example of an 'incomplete migration', as in Marek Okólski's view (Okólski, 2004), for the non-EU Eastern Europeans in Italy this is, on the contrary, a very elaborate modality of employment and mobility.

It is important here to mention that Italian policy actors are today, for the first time, confronting the issue of what I call circular care. This corresponds to the principle of job-sharing (*lavoro ripartito*). Yet the implementation of this hiring system still lacks useful and shared assessments based on an adequate number of cases. As a consequence, local welfare agencies, charity organizations and municipal or provincial offices are keen to acquire more knowledge on this topic in order to become able to orient employers and employees towards the most suitable arrangement. I should emphasize that circular care emerged as an important opportunity for the agency of a specific kind of working migrants, who seem to actively seek out this migratory pattern, as is evident in their request for support from their employers. In fact, circular care is the option often sought by migrant women to balance their personal desire to return home, the persistent financial dependency of their families, and the cutbacks on social security in post-Soviet countries. It is for women in these very specific circumstances that circularity has become a 'dream'.

3.5   Employability in Migrant Domestic Work

Employability is the key to understanding why and how each individual worker is able to step into a specific sector and subsequently move within it (Hillage & Pollard, 1999). McQuaid and Lindsay (2005) expand on this idea and show how being more employable means being able to put forward certain personal attributes together with some specific personal circumstances that can represent added value, enhancing one's labour opportunities. Workers have incorporated this urge to 'increase their employability' in their understanding of their own entry into and mobility within a specific labour sector. These transformations correspond to the fact that, since the EU Luxembourg Summit of 1997, the European labour market has changed substantially, not only in terms of new regulations that have been implemented but also – and this is what is of interest for the purposes of this chapter – with the emergence of new approaches to the meaning of work and to the experience of labourers. These new paradigms have rapidly become hegemonic in the way we understand the reasons behind employment versus unemployment, labour mobility and different forms of labour participation. It is becoming increasingly apparent that the workforce is required to be 'competitive' in order for individual workers to have better chances of selling themselves on the labour market. Being more competitive means being more flexible in terms of the time and location of the job, more adaptable to taking up different tasks, and offering a better price than others. Put differently, in this labour market with shrinking opportunities and almost no certainties, it is ultimately up to the worker to 'be more employable' (see Burroni et al., 2011; Crouch, 2008).

When it comes to flexible forms of employment, which started to be incorporated in EU labour legislation in 1997, the subjective acceptance of the need to take on (more) precarious work is crucial. People have resisted the risk of unemployment and consequent impoverishment by putting forward those capacities that make them fit for precarious work opportunities. They develop a 'proactive' attitude to engaging in temporary, long-distance, low-paid jobs. In this context, temporary precarious work is not only something that is imposed on workers by force, but (also) something that workers – given the scarcity of other, better employment opportunities – may actively seek. In this dynamic, personal factors act as stimuli for workers to make themselves available for flexible work. What interests me is the way these incentives are grounded in workers' personally constructed social characteristics in relation to how their gender, age, class and nationality simultaneously determine their opportunities in the labour market.

It is important to emphasize how this view runs counter to the perspective of previous studies on the impact of gender, age, nationality and ethnicity on labour market participation. For example, while dominant views on migrant worker participation focus on obstacles that they encounter due to their ethnicized background, migrants of specific nationalities can 'use' the ethnicization attached to their profiles in order to gain easier entry into some labour sectors (see Marchetti, 2014). In other words, some groups of workers may be more employable than others because of the expectations that relate to their constructed social identities. It is important to also consider the impact of gendered expectations on people's work trajectories, within the context of employability. Here again, scholars have tended to consider gendered features as a *burden* for the labour market participation of women, often excluding them from the job market and relegating them to part-time, low-paid jobs (Fredman, 2004; Jepsen, 2004). Without undermining the general argument concerning the gendered segregation in the labour market, my aim here is to shift the view by suggesting that gender could actually be seen as a *asset* for women to actively seek precarious and temporary jobs. Delving into the debate on employability shows how the 'language of employability' can describe the attitudes and the decisions taken by migrant women who step into home care work on temporary rather than permanent contracts.

Employability has been variously discussed and defined. One of the classic definitions is that by Jim Hillage and Emma Pollard, who understand employability as 'the capability to move self-sufficiently within the labour market to realize potential through sustainable employment' (Hillage & Pollard, 1999, p. 12). They add:

> For the individual, employability depends on the knowledge, skills and attitudes they possess, the way they use those assets and present them to employers and the context (e.g. personal circumstances and labour market environment) within which they seek work (ibid.).

According to this view, when a person is not able – for various possible reasons – to take a job and remains unemployed, it is said that this person 'is not employable' for that specific role. In other words, given a specific field of employment, employability relates to the ability of individuals to step into it or to change their role within it. As a consequence, policies on employability focus on the 'factors that allow or prevent' people from moving into suitable work.

Here we find that workers can use their personal skills and attitudes as assets in order to gain employment. Indeed, migrant women of specific nationalities can use the gendered and ethnicized attitudes about them (and their skills) to give them easier access to this labour sector (see Marchetti 2010). In other words, some groups of workers are more employable than others for certain jobs because of the social constructions that relate to their identities. This argument finds better support in another, more expanded, view of employability, namely the 'holistic approach to employability' of Ronald McQuaid and Colin Lindsay (2005). Such a holistic approach is vital, in my view, to making sense of the specific form of temporary circular labour migration that takes place in the Italian home care sector.

This combination of labour and migration patterns is the solution through which two (or more) women working in shifts are able to balance their emotional attachment to their families back home, their care commitments towards them, and the persistent financial dependency of these same women on their work abroad. By alternating at the workplace in Italy for periods of 3–4 months each, they are able to earn enough to financially support their households without having to be separated from them on a permanent basis. However, during this period they do not pay full taxes and social security contributions either in Italy or in their countries of origin, thus they end up being a full citizen 'neither here nor there', which is typical of circular migrants (Abrantes, 2013). In Marchetti (2013) I offer concrete examples of how workers organize their rotation in a way that resembles a job sharing arrangement at the international level.

Taking an employability perspective, we could say that it is only possible to 'become employable' as a circular carer when one possesses certain personal attributes. First of all, one needs to be proactive: to have a strong sense of initiative both in searching out a co-worker and an employer who will accept this arrangement. The ability to successfully couple with another woman is especially crucial. In the language of employability, circular carers have to be able to manage possible tensions with their co-workers, meet shared commitments, keep track of the calendar of arrivals and departures, teach tasks to the worker replacing them, and so on.

Secondly, they will have an advantage in this labour market if they are able to organize all of this, even from a distance, in the smoothest possible way for their employers and the care receiver. They must be able to use the telephone and internet in order to keep in touch with employers and co-workers during their absence, and also to solve unexpected problems and adapt to sudden needs. Fundamentally, they must have 'enhanced geographical mobility', that is, to be at ease with travelling long distances and crossing international borders (McQuaid & Lindsay, 2005).

As mentioned, in addition to such 'personal attributes', McQuaid and Linsday also consider it important to focus on personal circumstances to assess whether a worker is suitable for a specific job. Personal circumstances may be aspects of workers' (typically women's) personal lives that reduce their capacity to work, such as care and family commitments. Conversely, a personal circumstance that increases the employability of workers is related to their specific cultural background and the value of work within it.

3.6   The Role of Agencies and Intermediaries

The question of temporary migration in the provision of long-term care services, mainly for elderly and disabled people, is located at the meeting point between debates on the care and welfare regime and those on the migratory regime. In other words, to talk about the situation of temporary migrant care workers we need to look simultaneously at the regime that regulates the distribution of care provision between households, markets and states, and the regime concerning migrants' mobility and their conditions in the countries of arrival (Lutz & Palenga-Möllenbeck, 2011). The scholarly debate on these two different yet converging regimes has been vivid in recent years, focusing on the role of the different actors in this field and on the tendencies at play, so as to grasp different intersections of migratory and care regimes depending on the national setting, as Giulia Garofalo Geymonat, Anna Di Bartolomeo and myself have tried to do by comparing the role of agencies for migrant domestic workers in Germany and Taiwan (Marchetti et al., 2022).

It has been observed how in industrialized societies with ageing populations, a market logic in the field of long-term care provision is increasingly pervasive. As discussed in the previous chapter, companies are expanding their scope towards care provision, with goals more concerned with making profit and cutting costs, especially labour costs, than with the quality of the care provided (Farris & Marchetti, 2017). For Piper and Withers (2018), it is important to note how the commodification of care today clearly concerns not only the provision of care services as such, but all other elements of the process, such as the commercialization of the recruitment of care workers. Indeed, as we have seen, these steps of the process – usually performed by intermediaries and brokers – are a matter of monetary transaction and influenced by competitive market logic.

This market-oriented scenario creates a growing demand on a migrant labour force – women especially – employed at low wages and in precarious conditions (Ruhs and Anderson, 2010; Cangiano & Shutes, 2010). In this setting, transnational employment agencies support migrant women in the difficult goal of meeting the narrow requirements set by the labour and migration legislation of destination countries. Piper and Withers (2018) suggest the use of the term 'forced transnationalism' to express 'how the political and economic interests of sending and receiving countries coalesce to undermine migrants' rights to work (at home) and rights at work (abroad)' (p. 563). In their view, temporary care workers are forced transnational migrants for whom 'transnationalism is an involuntary experience defined by economic and social hardships that are endured in the absence of meaningful alternatives' (ibid.).

When it comes to the role of states, scholars argue that there is an increasing tendency by states to support the individual purchase of services from the care marketplace, rather than to provide them directly. This parallels the neoliberal reconfiguration of the role of the state as that of ensuring the functioning of markets, and the transformation of citizens into consumers individually responsible for their care needs (Anderson, 2012; Glendinning & Moran, 2009; Pavolini & Ranci, 2008).

Yet it is important to emphasize that if states have increasingly withdrawn from their role of direct care providers, they have strongly maintained the controlling one. First of all, states have an important (direct or indirect) regulatory function over these markets, since they provide the normative framework and the work regulations that allow private companies or individuals to offer their services to households. They can also determine the skills and profiles of migrants that can be recruited. Finally, the composition of the labour force will have a different character depending on the existing bilateral agreements – including pre-departure training programmes and quota-based policies – with workers' countries of origin, which are organized at the policy level (Kofman & Raghuram, 2015).

Against this background, as Tseng and Wang (2013) argue, states have been able to progressively delegate to employers (that is, care receivers) a series of important commitments and responsibilities that are vital to the functioning of the system. For this reason, resorting to agencies and brokers has become a pragmatic necessity for employers in order to overcome the practical and bureaucratic difficulties involved in the international recruitment of private care workers. This explains the booming number of agencies, brokers and intermediaries of various kinds who – legally or not – intervene in the recruitment of transnational care workers (Leiber et al., 2019; Schwiter et al., 2018). There is a growing debate among scholars whether these intermediaries are a good or a bad thing. Authors like Coe et al. 2010 see agencies as promoting further neoliberal deregulation of the care market and the precarization of work. Others like Lindquist et al. (2012) do not condemn these intermediaries and actually stress their importance in supporting and guiding workers who travel to a new country and enter this job market. Either way, the precarity of migrant care workers and their poor working conditions, especially in the case of temporary migrants, is at the centre of this discussion (Fudge & Strauss, 2013; McDowell et al., 2008).

References

Abrantes, M. (2013). Uncertain and experimental circularity: An investigation of the trajectories of migrant domestic Workers in Lisbon. *Journal of Immigrant & Refugee Studies, 11*(4), 384–400.

ACTRAV. (2013). *Decent work for domestic workers: The state of labour rights, social protection and trade union initiatives in Europe.* ILO.

Anderson, A. (2012). Europe's care regimes and the role of migrant care workers within them. *Journal of Population Ageing, 5*(2), 135–146.

Anderson, B., & Shutes, I. (2014). *Migration and care labour: Theory, policy and politics.* Palgrave Macmillan.

Bakan, A. B., & Stasiulis, D. (1994). Foreign domestic worker policy in Canada and the social boundaries of modern citizenship. *Science and Society, 58*(1), 7–33.

Boccagni, P., & Ambrosini, M. (2012). *Cercando il benessere nelle migrazioni: l'esperienza delle assistenti familiri straniere in Trentino.* Franco Angeli.

Bonifazi, C., & Marini, C. (2013). The impact of the economic crisis on foreigners in the Italian labour market. *Journal of Ethnic and Migration Studies, 40*(3), 1–19.

Brezzi, M., Dumont J.-C., Piacentini, M., & Thoreau, C. (2010). Determinants of localization of recent immigrants across OECD regions. *OECD workshop" migration and regional development*, Haziran-2010, Paris.

Burroni, L., Keune, M., & M. (2011). Flexicurity: A conceptual critique. *European Journal of Industrial Relations, 17*(1), 75–91.

Caglar, A., Sillo, T., & Jozwiak, I. (2011). *Circular migration between Ukraine and Hungary: Background report*. European University Institute.

Cangiano, A., & Shutes, I. (2010). Ageing, demand for care and the role of migrant care workers in the UK. *Population Ageing, 3*(1–2), 39–57.

Coe, N. M., Jones, K., & Ward, K. (2010). The business of temporary staffing: A developing research agenda. *Geography Compass, 4*(8), 1055–1068.

COM. (2007). 248 Final, On circular migration and mobility partnerships. Brussels.

Council of Europe. (2009). *The Stockholm programme: An open and secure Europe serving and protecting the citizens*. Document no. 17024/09, Brussels, 2 December 2009.

Cox, R. (2007). The au pair body: Sex object, sister or student? *European Journal of Women's Studies, 14*(3), 281–296.

Crouch, C. (2008). *The governance of labour market uncertainty: Towards a new research agenda*. Hugo Sinzheimer Institute.

Di Bartolomeo, A., & Marchetti, S. (2016). Migrant women's employment in paid reproductive work through the crisis: The case of Italy (2007–2012). *Investigaciones feministas, 7*, 57–74.

Ellis, M., Conway, D., & Bailey, A. J. (1996). The circular migration of Puerto Rican women: Towards a gendered explanation. *International Migration, 34*(1), 31–64.

Farris, S. R., & Marchetti, S. (2017). From the commodification to the corporatization of care: European perspectives and debates. *Social Politics: International Studies in Gender, State & Society, 24*(2), 109–131.

FRA. (2011). *Migrants in an irregular situation employed in domestic work: Fundamental rights challenges for the European Union and its member states*. FRA.

Fredman, S. (2004). Women at work: The broken promise of flexicurity. *Industrial Law Journal, 33*(4), 299–319.

Fudge, J., & Strauss, K. (2013). *Temporary work, agencies and unfree labour: Insecurity in the new world of work*. Routledge.

Gavanas, A. (2012). Migrant domestic workers, social network strategies and informal markets for domestic services in Sweden. *Women's Studies International Forum, 36*, 54–64. https://doi.org/10.1016/j.wsif.2012.08.004

Glendinning, C., & Moran, N. (2009). *Reforming long-term care: Recent lessons from other countries*. University of York, Social Policy Research Unity.

Gonzalez-Enriquez, C. (2013). Spain. In A. Triandafyllidou & R. Gropas (Eds.), *European immigration: A sourcebook* (pp. 339–351). Ashgate.

Hillage, J., & Pollard, E. (1999). Employability: Developing a framework for policy analysis. *Labour Market Trends, 107*, 83–84.

Hondagneu-Sotelo, P. (1994). Regulating the unregulated: Domestic workers' social networks. *Social Problems, 41*(50), 50–64.

Iglicka, K., Gmaj, K., & Borodzicz-Smolinski, W. (2011). *Circular migration patterns: Migration between Ukraine and Poland*. San Domenico di Fiesole. European University Institute.

Isaksen, L. W. (Ed.). (2010). *Global care work: Gender and migration in Nordic societies*. Nordic Academic Press.

Jepsen, M. (2004). Some reflections on a gender analysis of flexicurity. *Transfer: European Review of Labour and Research, 10*(2), 321–325.

Kindler, M. (2008). Risk and risk strategies in migration: Ukrainian domestic workers in Poland. In H. Lutz (Ed.), *Migration and domestic work: A European perspective on a global theme* (pp. 145–161). Ashgate.

Kofman, E., & Raghuram, P. (2015). *Gendered migrations and global social reproduction*. Palgrave Macmillan.

Lan, P. C. (2006). *Global Cinderellas: Migrant domestics and newly rich employers in Taiwan*. Duke University Press.

Leiber, S., Matuszczyk, K., & Rossow, V. (2019). Private labor market intermediaries in the Europeanized live-in care market between Germany and Poland: A typology. *Zeitschrift Für Sozialreform, 65*(3), 365–392.

Lendaro, A., & Imdorf, C. (2012). The use of ethnicity in recruiting domestic labour: A case study of French placement agencies in the care sector. *Employee Relations, 34*(6), 613–627.

Lindquist, J., Xiang, B., & Yeoh, B. S. A. (2012). Opening the black box of migration: Brokers, the organization of transnational mobility and the changing political economy in Asia. *Pacific Affairs, 85*(1), 7–19.

Lutz, H. (2011). *The new maids: Transnational women and the care economy*. Zed Books.

Lutz, H., & Palenga-Möllenbeck, E. (2011). Care, gender and migration: Towards a theory of transnational domestic work migration in Europe. *Journal of Contemporary European Studies, 19*(3), 349–364.

Massey, D. S., & Espinosa, K. (1997). What's driving Mexico-US migration? A theoretical, empirical, and policy analysis. *American Journal of Sociology, 102*(4), 939–999.

Massey, D. S., Arango, J., Hugo, G., Koaouci, A., Pellegrino, A., & Taylor, J. E. (1993). Theories of international migration: A review and appraisal. *Population and Development Review, 19*(3), 431–466.

Mai, N. (2011). *Reluctant circularities: The interplay between integration, return and circular migration within the Albanian migration to Italy*. European University Institute.

Marchetti, S. (2014). *Black girls: Migrant domestic workers and colonial legacies*. Brill.

Marchetti, S. (2017). Networks beyond nationalities? Relationships amongst Eastern European women workers in Italy facing the economic crisis. *Journal of Ethnic and Migration Studies, 43*(4), 633–651.

Marchetti, S., & Scrinzi, F. (2011). The gendered construction of a 'caring otherness'. In T. Caponio, F. Giordano, L. Ricaldone, & B. Manetti (Eds.), *World wide women Globalizzazione, Generi, Linguaggi – Vol. 3*. CIRSDe.

Marchetti, S. (2013). Dreaming circularity?. *Eastern European Women and Job-Sharing in Paid Home Care in Journal of Immigrant & Refugee Studies, 11*, 347–363 (ISSN 1556-2948).

Marchetti, S., & Venturini, A. (2014). Mothers and grandmothers on the move: Labour mobility and the household strategies of Moldovan and Ukrainian migrant women in Italy. *International Migration, 52*(5), 111–126.

Marchetti, S., Geymonat, G. G., & Di Bartolomeo, A. (2022). Dilemmas around temporariness and transnational recruitment agencies: The case of migrant caregivers in Taiwan and Germany. *Journal of Ethnic and Migration Studies*.

Marin, A., & Wellman, B. (2011). Social network analysis: An introduction. In J. Scott & P. J. Carrington (Eds.), *The SAGE handbook of social network analysis* (pp. 11–25). Sage.

Maroukis, T. (2013). Economic crisis and migrants' employment: A view from Greece in comparative perspective. *Policy Studies, 34*(2), 221–237.

Mazzacurati, C. (2005). Dal blat alla vendita del lavoro. Come sono cambiate colf e badanti ucraine e moldave a Padova. In T. Caponio & A. Colombo (Eds.), *Stranieri in Italia. Migrazioni globali, integrazioni locali*. il Mulino.

McDowell, L., Batnitzky, A., & Dyer, S. (2008). Internationalization and the spaces of temporary labour: The global assembly of a local workforce. *British Journal of Industrial Relations, 46*(4), 750–770.

McQuaid, R. W., & Lindsay, C. (2005). The concept of employability. *Urban Studies, 42*(2), 197–219.

Morokvasic, M. (1994). Pendeln statt auswandern. Das Beispiel der Polen. In M. Morokvasic & H. Rudolph (Eds.), *Wanderungsraum Europa: Menschen und Grenzen in Bewegung* (pp. 166–187). Stigma.

Novotny, J., & Hasman, J. (2015). The Emergence of Regional Immigrant Concentrations in USA and Australia: A Spatial Relatedness Approach. *PLoS ONE 10*(5). https://doi.org/10.1371/journal.pone.0126793

Okin, S. M. (1999). *Is multiculturalism bad for women?* Princeton University Press.

Okólski, M. (2004). The effects of political and economic transition on international migration in central and Eastern Europe. In D. S. Massey & J. E. Taylor (Eds.), *International migration: Prospects and policies in a global market* (pp. 35–58). Oxford University Press.

Parreñas, R. S. (2001). *Servants of globalization: Women, migration and domestic work.* University Press.

Parreñas, R. S. (2010). Homeward bound: The circular migration of entertainers between Japan and the Philippines. *Global Networks, 10*(3), 301–323.

Pavolini, E., & Ranci, C. (2008). Restructuring the welfare state: Reforms in long-term care in western European countries. *Journal of European Social Policy, 18*(3), 246–259.

Piper, N., & Withers, M. (2018). Forced transnationalism and temporary labour migration: Implications for understanding migrant rights. *Identities, 25*(5), 558–575.

Pool, C., (2003). Hedendaagse migratie van Polen naar Nederland. *Justitiële verkenningen, 29*(4), 63–80.

Ruhs, M., & Anderson, B. (2010). *Who needs migrant workers? Labour shortages, immigration, and public policy.* University Press.

Schrover, M., Van der Leun, J., & Chris Q. (2007). Niches, labour market segregation, ethnicity and gender. *Journal of Ethnic and Migration Studies 33*(4), 529–540. https://doi.org/10.1080/13691830701265404

Schwiter, K., Berndt, C., & Truong, J. (2018). Neoliberal austerity and the marketisation of elderly care. *Social & Cultural Geography, 19*(3), 379–399.

Scrinzi, F. (2013). *Genre, migrations et emplois de care en France et en Italie. Construction de la non qualification et de l'altérité ethnique.* Editions Pétra.

Solari, C. (2010). Resource drain vs. constitutive circularity: Comparing the gendered effects of post-soviet migration patterns in Ukraine. *Anthropology of East Europe Review, 28*, 215–238.

Spijkerboer, T., & Van Walsum, S. (Eds.). (2007). *Women and immigration law: New variations on classical feminist themes.* Routledge.

Timonen, V., & Doyle, M. (2010). Migrant care workers' relationships with care recipients, colleagues and employers. *European Journal of Women's Studies, 17*(1), 25–41.

Triandafyllidou, A. (2011). *Circular migration between the EU and its neighbours: A comparative analysis.* European University Institute.

Triandafyllidou, A. (Ed.). (2013). *Irregular migrant domestic workers in Europe: Who cares?* Ashgate.

Triandafyllidou, A., & Marchetti, S. (2014). *Europe 2020: Addressing low skill labour migration at times of fragile recovery.* Robert Schuman Centre for Advanced Studies Research Paper No. RSCAS.

Triandafyllidou, A., & Marchetti, S. (Eds.). (2015). *Employers, agencies and immigration: Care work in Europe.* Ashgate.

Tseng, Y., & Wang, H. (2013). Governing migrant Workers at a Distance: Managing the temporary status of Guestworkers in Taiwan. *International Migration, 51*(4), 1–19.

Vasey, H. (2015). Trajectories of migration, social networks and emergent landscapes of migrant work. *Migration Studies, 4*(1), 76–96.

Vianello, F. A. (2009). *Migrando sole. Legami transnazionali tra Ucraina e Italia.* Franco Angeli.

Vietti, F. (2010). *Il paese delle badanti.* Meltemi.

Chapter 4
Inequalities

4.1 The Intersectionality of Inequalities and Migrant Domestic Work

In parallel with the development of the scholarship on migrant domestic work, the feminist approach of intersectionality of differences has gained traction in the social sciences in recent decades. I do not have the space here to account for the different understandings of intersectionality and their methodological implications for research (see Collins & Bilge, 2020; Lutz et al., 2016; Romero, 2017). Certainly the fact that some of the sociologists occupied with domestic workers' issues have also used intersectionality in their work (for instance Helma Lutz in Germany, and Mary Romero in the US) has had profound repercussions. An intersectional approach requires that we avoid homogenizing views on people's experiences, and seek a deeper understanding of the real elements of commonality or difference between them. In other words, an intersectional perspective tells us that between people who apparently share the same experience, or the same social conditions, there may also be key differences. In the study of migrant domestic work this occurs at two different levels.

First of all, we need to draw attention to the disparity *between* migrant domestic workers due to their different nationalities, age, legal status, and so forth, since this has an impact on their particular trajectories. This also helps us to make sense of the experiences of the many migrant men, of various nationalities, who perform paid domestic work. A major part of the literature on migrant domestic workers discussed in this book is based on understanding how their labour conditions are affected by differences in their migratory experience, nationality and citizenship status, gender, age, and so on.

Moreover, adopting an intersectional perspective on domestic workers' experiences also means highlighting the differences that exist *within* this labour market, in which some workers have a more privileged position to others. For example, we know that notions of ethnicity and gender are embedded and reproduced in

© The Author(s) 2022
S. Marchetti, *Migration and Domestic Work*, IMISCOE Research Series,
https://doi.org/10.1007/978-3-031-11466-3_4

recruitment and training practices undertaken by employment agencies or by companies that provide care services. More particularly, training activities are based on essentialist gendered assumptions about the 'traditional culture' of migrant women and on an idealized view of family relations in their home countries. For instance, care providers' managers have to deal with the clients' preferred choice of caregivers from specific ethnic, religious or national backgrounds, and sometimes with their hostility towards others that do not fulfil their expectations.

Another example of difference that exists *within* this labour market concerns the division between workers who do live-in and those who do live-out jobs. This differentiation between employment often corresponds to an intersectional hierarchy between workers due to their racialized backgrounds, their citizenship rights in the host country, the level of gendered commitments towards the family of origin, and so forth. In fact, live-in jobs are considered to be more strenuous are often taken up by women (or men) who, due to their personal characteristics have fewer opportunities in the labour market. They usually consist of full-time assistance to elderly people or children in their homes, based on private arrangements. Elderly care receivers often have mental disorders, and many require a 24 h watch. In addition to this personal care, live-in workers are also responsible for cleaning the house, gardening, and shopping. These workers often lament their reduced free time, and the feeling that they are completely absorbed by the family life of the person they assist. It is also true, however, that these jobs allow workers to save most of their salary, which usually goes towards remittances for families back home, since food and accommodation are provided by employers (see Boccagni & Ambrosini, 2012, pp. 35–39).

On the other side, live-out work is often considered a better opportunity for migrant domestic workers who are in a more empowered position to the others. Live-out work is generally more diversified than live-in work. It might consist of a cleaning job done on an hourly basis, babysitting, or elder care provided only during the day. It is true that live-out jobs are more disadvantageous than live-in in terms of income, since live-out workers must pay for their food, accommodation and transportation. Yet, these women can start living on their own and can therefore host their husbands and children. They can also start to develop interests and occupations beside work, including cultural and political activities. Women who work this way are defined by Pasquinelli and Rusmini (2013) as the 'new generation' of care workers, who prioritize their independence and free time over the commitment to save money to support their families in the home country.

Along the same lines, another example of a difference within this workforce which can be seen in a intersectional perspective, is that between those who work in the traditional household-based domestic service sector and those who are in bureaucratized home care in the non-profit sector, the latter constituting a form of professional and social mobility for migrant women. Workers in these jobs have the opportunity to work in a team and to participate in the tutoring and supervision offered by some cooperatives. Most of the caregivers employed by the cooperatives hold a formal qualification. These advantages compensate for the poor working conditions and the stress for caregivers to move from one client's place to another several times during the working day. Here again we see that, as with 'migrant domestic workers', behind the general description there is a very nuanced picture which concerns several intersecting personal characteristics, including the educational and professional profile of these migrant labourers.

4.2   Beyond Sisterhood: Relationships with Employers

Another important use of intersectionality in migrant domestic work is to challenge the supposed commonality between workers and employers by virtue of both being women (as discussed in Chap. 2). This element of commonality is questioned by the many differences and the hierarchical positioning between these two groups of women, workers and employers. In the following pages, we will see the different aspects of this differentiation and how this takes place in the relationship between the two subjects.

In order to address the relationship between migrant domestic workers and their employers we need to start from the acknowledgment that employers are themselves a varied group: they are people of various ages and family situations, with diverse professional and educational backgrounds, living in the most industrialized and urban areas as well as in rural areas and small towns. They may be university professors or housewives, factory workers or lawyers. Yet, a crucial determinant remains that of gender. The relevance of women's predominance among employers is to be seen within a general feminization in the realm of paid care: it is usually daughters and mothers who take up the role of the 'employer' within the family unit when it comes to employing a babysitter for the children or a caregiver for an elderly parent. Within the couple, although men participate in some ways, women are still the ones mainly in charge of the employment and personal relationship with the person they have hired. Thus, paid domestic work is a gendered sector not only regarding employees but also regarding employers.

As we have already seen, the inequality affecting the dyad employer-employee challenges notions of 'sisterhood' between women, especially when we consider the asymmetry between the employer as a full citizen and the worker as an 'alien' or temporary citizen (Barua et al., 2017; Marchetti, 2016). Feminist scholars have also discussed the unequal distribution of reproductive labour *between* women, since this can often be delegated from middle-class women onto women from working class and racialized groups (Nakano Glenn, 1996). It is important to consider the difference in the dyad when domestic workers are migrants in industrialized countries. The differentiation and hierarchy *between* women involved in reproductive labour builds on a view which considers these tasks more 'naturally' suitable for the most vulnerable and stigmatized subjects (Gutiérrez-Rodríguez, 2010). The social construction of care-giving jobs as non-skilled relies on the dualism between cleaning and other material tasks on the one hand, and care and emotional work on the other. For example, empirical studies (Anderson, 2000) have shown that private employers of migrant domestic workers emphasize the cleaning tasks accomplished by their employees, while obscuring their emotional and care work. Yet, Bridget Anderson invokes the image of Dr. Jekyll and Mr. Hyde to explain how employers and employees are still united by interdependent representations linked to domesticity and housework. While domestic workers perform heavy jobs, middle-class employers have the role of organizing that job: they carefully choose the best employee, they assign her the tasks to fulfil and give her instructions regarding the education of the children. Therefore, employers are somehow 'domestic' but without also being 'dirty'. Domestic workers represent the physicality and dirtiness of domestic work, while the employers confirm their superiority in feminine and domestic skills (Anderson, 2000).

On the same issue, Julia Kristeva (1980) and Douglas and Isherwood (1979) spoke of 'abjection' to describe how middle-class women dismiss the low-level domestic tasks, which are considered repulsive and demeaning, in order to achieve the ideal of respectable women (Mosse, 1985). This emerging dichotomy in female models has been associated with new women's figures such as what Daniel Adeoyé Leslie (1993) has called the 'new traditionalist model' who is devoted to their husbands and children, yet in a bourgeois fashion. Nicky Gregson and Michelle Lowe in their classic book *Servicing the Middle Class* acknowledge that 'in certain middle-class households cleaning is no longer being seen as a suitable use of middle-class women's time-space. … Social transformations … have restructured women's relations to the home in ways that have altered their traditional ties to domesticity' (Gregson & Lowe, 1994, p. 24).

The role of employers is a matter of discussion in the debate on paid domestic work. Research on employers shows the importance of understanding how they elaborate on their need for 'help' with caring and cleaning, how they relate to their 'employees', and how they negotiate tensions in their daily family and working lives (Triandafyllidou & Marchetti, 2015). Interesting elements emerge from interviews with employers, which give a complicated account of the experience of 'paying for care', such as for example mothers' personal conflict between their parenting models and their work commitments, as well as adult daughters' conflict between the commitment to care for their elderly parents and the desire to break free from such family obligations.

In a comparative analysis, it is also important to consider how the role of employers changes depending on the overall arrangements relating to care and domestic work. Maurizio Ambrosini (2015) discusses the tendency of family members (mothers and daughters in particular) no longer being providers of care, but rather more akin to 'care managers' who organize the job of those actually performing the care tasks. It is in this management dimension that they also become employers.

More generally, while in the past the employment of a cleaner, housekeeper, carer, nanny, or general domestic helper was a luxury that few households could afford, over the last couple of decades employers have increasingly come from the middle and lower middle classes; for them to employ someone is not a luxury but a necessity (Triandafyllidou & Marchetti, 2015). The domestic worker fills the gaps created by a changing family structure, a diminishing welfare state, an ageing society, and most importantly, increased participation of women in the labour market.

In Triandafyllidou and Marchetti (2015), we discuss the various types of paid domestic work and the different categories of employers, with specific attention to the socio-economic features that characterize them as a group. Thus we argue that employers can be categorized depending on:

(a) the type of services they require: cleaning, care, other household chores such as gardening or grocery shopping; or a combination of these
(b) their relationship with the employee: are they the direct recipient of services, or are they engaging the care worker or cleaner on behalf of someone else, such as an elderly parent?
(c) the type of work arrangement that they request: a live-in, paid worker on a monthly basis; or a paid worker on an hourly or daily wage
(d) their family situation: they may include parents (or a single parent) with young children (in need of babysitting and help with cleaning), elderly people who are self-sufficient but need help cleaning and caring for themselves; the 'sandwich' generation of people who are in their 60s with grown children still in the home and with very elderly parents (in their 90s) in need of care assistance; they may include dual career families with or without young children.

The combination of type of work, type of family, work arrangements and relationships with employees produces several schemes and types of paid domestic work that may veer more into the care profession or more into cleaning and house or garden chores.

Furthermore, employers of paid domestic workers may be classed into two main categories: 'employers as agents of social change' and 'employers as preservers of traditions' (Triandafyllidou & Marchetti, 2015). For the first category, the (partial) delegation of their care tasks to paid workers is a way for them to pursue new models of parenthood and family life, which do not entail a long daily physical commitment towards their family members. Goñalons-Pons (2015) talks about the search for a 'modern' version of domesticity that combines the responsibility towards loved ones with engagement in paid work and a professional career, which inevitably reduces the amount of time spent in the home.

It is interesting to look at the role of employers of paid domestic workers to acquire a different yet often complementary view of the experiences of domestic workers and the context of those experiences. It is an important perspective which has generally been overlooked, with employers remaining at the fringes of the policy debate on domestic work and on the employment of migrants in the care and cleaning sector. In some countries, certain employers' organizations have been playing an important role in negotiating rights and social status for domestic workers, often acting as allies of the workers' organizations against the state and private market actors. There is a strong need to strengthen and extend this capacity of employers to more countries (Box 4.1).[1]

---

[1] On the importance of employers' organizations see several contributions by activists, in the 'Open Democracy: Beyond Trafficking and Slavery' policy debate guest edited by Eileen Boris, Jennifer Fish, Giulia Garofalo Geymonat and myself: 'Beyond "maids and madams": can employers be allies in new policies for domestic workers' rights?' (Boris et al., 2018).

Box 4.1: Types of Employers
We can distinguish employers of paid domestic workers into two main categories (Triandafyllidou & Marchetti, 2015). We can call the first category 'employers as agents of social change', which includes employers such as the working mothers of young children or the daughters of elderly parents. For these individuals, hiring a domestic worker, babysitter or elder carer is a way to pursue new models of parenthood and family life that lightens their overall workload by reducing their family commitments. One may talk of the search for a 'modern' version of domesticity that combines responsibilities towards loved ones with paid work and a professional career, inevitably reducing the amount of time spent as the *materfamilias* in the home.

The second category of employers are the 'preservers of tradition' and it includes those who have to delegate the actual performance of care and domestic work to paid workers, but who would probably prefer to do the work themselves. Employing someone is a second best option, but it comes at the cost of also feeling guilt or betrayal. This type of employer expresses discomfort in the employment relationship. In so doing, they put forward traditional views on commitment towards their households.

However, for either category, particularly when there is no clear and practical regulation of the sector, it is easy to go down the path of violating workers' rights. Such problems are barely addressed by stricter regulation of the sector, as this often has the opposite effect of causing employer families to avoid registration and regulation altogether.

4.3   The Legacy of Slavery and Colonialism

The way we talk today about social divisions (gender, age, class, 'race'/ethnicity and so on) cannot be fully understood without considering the historical context in which they have been shaped. This brings our attention to colonialism, seen as a political and economic project which was accompanied by a process of cultural, social, and moral categorization. A postcolonial perspective can enrich our understanding of the division of care work at the global level.

In some countries, the differences between women as employers, and employees in particular, are strongly inflected by the legacies of slavery and of colonial domination (Ally, 2009; Marchetti, 2014; Masi de Casanova et al., 2018; Ribeiro Corossacz, 2018). A racialization of social differences is still evident in contemporary societies, and it is of the utmost importance in the relationship between employer and employee. This is for example when the former belongs to the privileged urban middle class and the latter is a racialized woman from a rural background living on the outskirts of a major city, or when women from an indigenous background work for households belonging to the ethnically/racially privileged group (Haskins, 2001). It also contributes to shaping what Evelyn Nakano Glenn (1996) calls the 'racial division of paid reproductive labor'.

Relationships between 'black maids' and 'white mistresses' in the historical context of slavery and racial segregation have been discussed for example by Phyllis Palmer (1983, 1989) speaking about the relationships between US middle-class white women and their African American maids between 1920 and 1945. Jaqueline Cock (1989) has investigated the relationships between white employers and their black domestic workers in South Africa during Apartheid. Also in the Latin American context, differences between women as employers or employees are strongly inflected by colonial legacies and internal migrations. The corresponding racialization of social differences is still evident in Latin American societies in the disparity between different areas (for instance, former plantations vs colonial capital cities), and in the social stratifications in urban settings. For Jenny Sharpe, this legacy consists in a constant, albeit unmentioned, presence of what she calls the 'ghost of slavery' (Sharpe, 2003).

A specifically European version of this debate must take into account the fact that large numbers of migrants arrived from former colonies in the 1960s to the 1980s. These migrants' experiences were characterized by an intense pre-migratory relationship with their country of arrival. Depending on the context, this relationship was reflected in the level of their citizenship rights, in the language they spoke, or in their previous knowledge about their destination country, which until recently had been ruling their own. However, acknowledging these connections has been far from reciprocal since the former colonizers are often not equally aware or willing to acknowledge the legacy of colonial times (Marchetti, 2014).

The experience of postcolonial domestic workers is determined by the *continuity* between the time 'before' and 'after' colonization, as before and after the migration. The employer-employee dualism descends from a pattern inaugurated in the colonial setting, where the normative character of the relationship between native women and bourgeois Europeans was established. The emergence of these characteristics sets the case of women coming from former colonies to work in the land of the former colonizers apart as unique, or at least as very different from the experience of other groups. In Marchetti (2014), I demonstrated that representations attached to postcolonial migrant women led to contrasting endings: they eased their entrance into the former colonizers' society but, at the same time, they relegated them to the lowest strata of that same society. These women have been living a life on the edge of this *ambivalence*, where being postcolonial migrants was simultaneously their tool of resistance, and the reason for their subordination. Postcoloniality, in this sense, is a double-sided relationship between colonized and colonizers, oscillating between a positive recognition and a strangling tie. We can see a continuity between colonization and globalization, between colonial regimes and contemporary paid domestic work, and finally, between the colonial white mistress and black servant dichotomy and the relationship between native and migrant women in Europe today. Domestic workers had learned caring and nurturing skills during their youth, therefore shaped under colonial legacies, in which gender and class features are combined with 'race' (Box 4.2).

Box 4.2: Selling a 'Caring Otherness'
One of the many examples of how workers and agencies manipulate gendered constructions of caregiving, making it more suitable for specific categories of women (and not for others) comes from the history of paid home care in the Netherlands. This setting was fundamentally created by employment agencies that were especially active in the 1970s and 1980s. Their racialized assumptions about caregiving is important both in the recruitment practices and the differentiation between co-workers.

In the stories I collected (Marchetti, 2014), these agencies' managers were literally encouraging Afro-Surinamese women to 'take advantage of their background', thus promoting an essentialist image of Surinamese women as particularly gifted in the care of the elderly. In other words, the agencies were emphasizing that 'Surinamese culture' had something to offer to Dutch society: Surinamese women's marketable caring skills. In so doing they encouraged the creation of a labour niche based on specific gendered and racialized representations. In this context, the agencies thus performed a mediation, not only at the economic level, but also at the cultural level, in the encounter between demand and supply. In practical terms, the agencies appreciated a form of education that was rather common among Afro-Surinamese women, such as studies related to sanitation, infancy or housekeeping. Secondly, they promoted representations emphasizing 'respect' for elderly people as a racialized characteristic of Surinamese society which is a common essentialist belief.

These attitudes also correspond to the narratives about the competition between Afro-Surinamese and Dutch caregivers regarding their respective caring abilities, based on different characteristics perceived to be typical of both groups. The first narrative refers again to the allegedly more respectful attitude of the Surinamese than the Dutch. A second theme is the question of cleanliness, as Afro-Surinamese care givers often complain about the poor hygiene of their Dutch colleagues. This last point is very interesting as far as it shows Surinamese women's attempts to dismantle the perceived superiority of their white colleagues and rehabilitate their own background in racialized terms. Finally, interviewees stressed their emotional involvement in caregiving, in contrast with the colder and money-orientated attitudes of the Dutch. For the Afro-Surinamese interviewees, the focus was on the relationship with the patients as a continuous practice of overcoming difficult situations to gain the trust of the recipients of care.

4.4   Citizenship and Belonging

The burgeoning debate that has flourished around the notion of citizenship in recent years has resulted in many and often contrasting definitions (Isin et al., 2013). Citizenship has been seen as something 'flexible' (Ong, 1999), as a 'lived' experience (Hall & Williamson, 1999) or as the result of 'acts' of citizenship (Isin & Nielsen, 2008). Additionally, it has been seen as a multi-layered 'package' of practices, rights and identities that is composed in different ways depending on the historical and geographical context (Joppke, 2007; Yuval-Davis, 1999). As Sandro Mezzadra (2006) emphasizes, migrants' stories address the question of rights and legal entitlements, but they also go beyond the mere institutional dimension of citizenship. It is in this sense that citizenship is an object of negotiation: it is a field in which people with different positions and different trajectories enact their strategies for the acquisition of better status and thus renegotiate social boundaries between them. Finally, it is also important to mention the feminist debate on citizenship, which has concentrated on the measure in which *all* women are, by definition, excluded by the concepts of citizenship, justice and democracy in modern nation states (e.g., Fraser, 2003; Lister et al., 2007; Mouffe, 1992; Young, 1990).

The exclusion of migrant domestic workers from citizenship rights has attracted the attention of several political and social scientists (Bosniak, 2008; Lutz, 2011; Ong, 2006; Sarti, 2005; Triandafyllidou, 2013). Others have focused on this group's social mobilization to claim access to more citizenship rights in their countries of residence (Constable, 2009; Gutiérrez-Rodríguez, 2010). Others have spoken about a 'partial citizenship' (Bauböck, 2011; Parreñas, 2001) for migrants, a notion which is particularly apt to describe the differences between domestic workers and their employers. The idea of a 'partiality' of citizenship indeed emphasizes hat there are various degrees and forms of access to citizenship entitlements. Against this background, it is not only that domestic workers and their employers have different degrees of access (the first as migrants versus the latter as non-migrants) but there is also a difference *among* workers based on their different migratory statuses (temporary, permanent, undocumented and so on). This is, in turn, crucially conditioned by national legislation on migration, labour and citizenship rights.

A lack of citizenship rights for migrant workers, resulting from being either temporary or undocumented migrants in Europe, influences their relationship with female employers. This can be seen, for instance, in 'maternalistic' attitudes that are frequently at play in relationships between migrant employees and non-migrant employers. One example of it is the use of the expression 'being part of the family' – interchangeably used by employers and employees alike – and which has been a recurrent topic of analysis in studies on paid domestic work in different contexts (Lan, 2006; Locher-Scholten, 2000; Parreñas, 2001; Ray & Qayum, 2009; Rothenberg, 2000). Reference to being part of the family, as applied to people who are *not* family members, has been called the 'family analogy'. The frequent use of this analogy on the part of both employers and employees has animated a large part of the scholarly debate on paid domestic work. Scholarly texts, but also personal memoirs, novels, and films on the topic of paid domestic work question whether or not domestic workers can be equated to members of the families for whom they work.

Opinions on this issue vary greatly. Some scholars find the use of the family analogy to be one of the most pervasive forms of control and exploitation operating in this labour sector (Lan, 2006; Ray & Qayum, 2009), especially in the context of nationalist and colonialist discourses (Anderson, 2014; Kofman, 2005;

Locher-Scholten, 2000). Other scholars conversely see the use of the family analogy as a positive element that offers workers an opportunity to express intimacy with and closeness to their employers (Näre, 2012; Parreñas, 2001).

Within this larger debate on family-based narratives of paid domestic work, the question of maternalism has attracted the attention of those who are specifically interested in employer-employee interactions as examples of negotiations between women across racial and/or socio-economic hierarchies.

In her pioneering book on African American domestic workers in Boston, Judith Rollins (1985) devotes a chapter to 'deference and maternalism'. Her focus is the legacy of ancient forms of servitude in contemporary paid domestic work. Rollins says that in ancient Rome, servants were depicted as childlike, irresponsible, and lacking autonomy; they lived under the responsibility of their master, the 'father of the house' (*paterfamilias*), who was accountable for them, extracting service and loyalty in exchange for protection. In her view, a similar pattern applies today to the employment of paid domestic workers, wherein women are typically hired, instructed, and controlled by other women. For Rollins, maternalistic attitudes can be seen in the tendency of employers, who are women in positions constructed as racially and socio-economically superior, to seek 'deference and gratitude' on the part of domestic workers. Their generous and charitable gestures provide a confirmation of their higher status. For this reason, 'maternalism may protect and nurture, [but] it also degrades and insults' (Rollins, 1985: 186). In other words, 'maternalistic employers' are those who, albeit unconsciously, while helping and protecting their employees, confirm their inferiority and by extension, that of all people belonging to their social category (migrants, black people, poor people, and so on).

The topic of helpful gestures and feelings of gratitude between employers and employees also connects to previous studies in this field concerning the meaning of the gifts that employers typically give to domestic workers. Scholars have been quite divided on this issue. Jacqueline Cock, for example, is very critical of this practice, saying 'Gifts help to reinforce the social hierarchy by promoting feelings of loyalty, faithfulness and gratitude. … This kind of paternalist relationship is intensively demeaning for the dependent servant' (Cock, 1989: 82). Mary Romero (1992: 152) and Elaine Kaplan (1987) are equally critical of gift-giving as a strategy that ultimately damages domestic workers. Other scholars are less critical, as is Rhacel Parreñas, who takes the standpoint of many Filipina domestic workers who 'have gained tremendous material benefits from the inclination of employers to give gifts' (Parreñas, 2001: 187).

Turning to more recent scholarship, a Filipina scholar, Janet Arnado, takes up the concept of maternalism and uses it in her analysis of interviews held in Manila, where domestic workers are mainly young women migrating from rural areas to the city (Arnado, 2003). Arnado identifies four types of maternalism that Filipina employers adopt in relation to their employees. These are:

1. maternalism as a 'part of the family' ideology (which is essentially Rollins' view of maternalism);
2. maternalism as a form of emotional labour;

3. maternalism to enhance the worker's social network; and finally
4. maternalism based on the value of *utang na loob* (a 'debt of gratitude').

Maternalism between migrant employees and their non-migrant employers, although it might bring workers some immediate benefits, is ultimately detrimental to the workers. This is because this maternalism brings with it a series of stereotypical representations, such as that of migrant women as victims of their own decisions to migrate, or transnational mothers as suffering figures, which promote an image of migrant domestic workers as vulnerable and needy subjects, dependent on the goodwill of helpful employers.

4.5 Migrant Domestic Workers and Economic Crisis

After the 2008 financial and economic crisis, scholars were concerned about the possible impact of the recession on labour sectors where migrants were employed. The fear was that working class non-migrant workers would start to compete with migrants for jobs which they had previously dismissed, but which they might want to take up to face the new dire economic necessities. This competition would be likely to be very 'gendered', since both migrant and non-migrant women would strive for the lower-scale jobs, mainly in the service sector.

There is a long-standing debate on whether women are a 'reserve army', meaning that they enter paid work in times of economic expansion, but retreat into unemployment and home life in times of economic contraction (Milkman, 1976). However, scholars have shown how during the Great Depression, as well as the Asian financial crisis in 1997, women's labour participation did not meet this expectation (Lim, 2000). Women's labour participation in times of recession and shrinking opportunities seems to be quite unpredictable, since it depends on the specific configuration of the labour markets in each context, and women's potential complementarity or competition with other workers (men, migrants, and so on).

Rubery and Rafferty (2013) took up this question while looking at women's labour participation (versus that of men) in the 2008 crisis in the United Kingdom. They found that patterns of sectorial gender segregation were crucial in measuring female employment. They concluded that the condition of these women workers was extremely volatile, and that no sector is inevitably 'protected'. External forces may cause job loss and employment downgrading even in fields that are traditionally seen as 'safe'.

As regards migrant women in the care and domestic sector, however, other authors have observed that in countries such as Italy they certainly had fewer problems keeping their jobs than migrant men, employed in other sectors (Bonifazi & Marini, 2013; Pastore et al., 2013; Reyneri, 2010). This is true in countries where migrant women tend to be employed in specific labour market niches, especially reproductive work. In fact, paid domestic and care work emerged as a relatively 'safe' sector, protected by the dynamics provoked by the financial crisis of those years (ISTAT, 2013; Semenza, 2012).

Along the same lines, Sara Farris (2015) has discussed the factors that determine the general stability in the occupation of migrant women as domestic and care workers between 2007 and 2011. She found that the main determinant was the non-cyclical character of this sector, since regardless of general economic trends, the demand for personal care services is always high due to an ageing European population. This sector has also remained almost exclusively occupied by migrants due to its 'very severe, unregulated, stigmatized and poor working conditions' (Farris, 2015: 12). Thus, she defines domestic and care workers as a 'regular' rather than a 'reserve' army, to emphasize the chronic need for these occupations in European societies.

If we look more closely, it is important to identify the elements of change and continuity for migrant women in the labour market through the crisis. This can be done by looking at elements of *complementarity* and *competition* with other workers' groups, both in ethnic terms (foreign women versus native women) and in gender terms (foreign women versus foreign men) (Di Bartolomeo & Marchetti, 2016). In other words, it is important to see whether migrant women compete with or rather complement non-migrant women and migrant men in the labour market, and whether these patterns changed during the recession. Looking at Italy between 2007 and 2021, in Di Bartolomeo and Marchetti (2016) we demonstrated what we call an 'ethnic complementarity' between Italian and foreign women. Migrant and Italian women complement each other, as they are employed in different occupations within the same sector, or they are performing different tasks within the same occupation. This difference is what determines a permanent demand for a low-paid, flexible, and highly gendered workforce, ready to be employed by Italian households when the need arises.

4.6   Migrant Domestic Workers in the Covid-19 Pandemic

The Covid-19 pandemic in the spring of 2020 shattered the globe. Domestic and care workers were one of the categories most affected by the pandemic at the international level (ILO, 2020; Marchetti & Boris, 2020; Rosińska & Pellerito, 2022). These workers were in a quite vulnerable situation, since they both carried a high risk of contracting or transmitting the disease in their contact with the fragile people they assisted, and risked losing work and payment. This was particularly the case for personal caregivers. The scenario was even more worrisome for migrants in a precarious position due to restrictions on their citizenship rights, their rights to family reunification, and their access to social and health services and other forms of support. In Europe, such concern also applied to the many EU migrants moving from Eastern countries to the West for work, and which comprise the majority of those employed in the domestic and care sector, especially in the case of women.

In June 2020, the ILO estimated that 55 million domestic workers were at risk of being significantly impacted by Covid-19 (ILO, 2020), where 'significantly impacted' meant a reduction in the number of hours of work and earnings, as well as job losses. According to the estimates, in Northern, Western, and Southern Europe, 50% of domestic workers were significantly impacted by the pandemic. In Marchetti and Mesiäislehto (2022) we examine the employment and working hours of domestic workers after the 2020 pandemic outbreak by using data from the EU Labour Force Survey.[2] During spring 2020, employment in paid domestic work dropped dramatically, particularly in Spain, where the sector employed 90,000 fewer people after the first quarter, and in Italy (73,000 fewer people). The relative change in employment between 2019 and 2020 was high in all seven countries, with a 16–24% drop in 1 year. At the same time, the change in working hours of those employed varied. Compared to 2019, the relative change in 2020 was most significant in Portugal and Poland with around 10% fewer hours worked, while in other countries the change was minor. The short-term negative changes at the beginning of the pandemic were most visible in France and Portugal and some changes were also observed in the UK and the Netherlands.

Research and reports on migrant care workers suggest that the social and economic consequences of the Covid-19 crisis were particularly difficult for circular migrants who, due to travel restrictions, had to either extend their stay in the country where they worked, or remain in their home country without income (Leiblfinger et al., 2020; Leichsenring et al., 2020). Those who extended their stay were reported to frequently have to work for weeks without days off. The uncertainty of the situation and how long it might last was also a mental and emotional strain, for example for personal care workers who spent weeks in isolation with a sick person (Leichsenring et al., 2020).

However, the strong dependency on the migrant workforce, particularly in elder care, led some governments to take measures to ensure the inflow of migrants in the care sector (Kuhlmann et al., 2020). For example in Romania, nearly 200 chartered flights left Romania for other countries in Europe at a time when scheduled flights were cancelled (Mutler, 2020). In addition, transportation was organized for care workers working with the elderly by trains departing from Timişoara to Vienna (Cretan & Light, 2020).

Unfortunately, the support they received was limited by the 'partial citizen' status we discussed before: even if they are regular residents and registered workers, they might not fulfil the bureaucratic requirements to apply for state subsidies. For example, as Michael Leiblfinger, Karin Schwiter, Helma Lutz and others explain, in Austria care workers were unable to access Covid-19 support, which would require them to have an Austrian tax number and bank account (Leiblfinger et al., 2020). Likewise in Germany, migrant care workers were excluded from benefits because

---

[2]The data available in the Eurostat database does not provide disaggregated information on employment by occupation, which is why domestic workers are here defined as persons employed by private households that refers to the NACE (European industry standard classification system) category 'activities of households as employers of domestic personnel' (see ILO, 2011).

they are usually posted workers under the EU directive, or self-employed and paying taxes in their home countries (ibid.).

There are also cases in which governments have explicitly targeted migrants and/
or domestic and care workers in their interventions. For example, the French government adopted compensation mechanisms for domestic and care workers, asking
their employers to pay them for hours not worked, and it has reimbursed them 80%
of their cost, on the condition that they keep the employment in place. In Belgium,
both the Walloon and Brussels governments required domestic and care workers to
stop working. Forms of 'corona unemployment' subsidies applied to domestic and
care workers who must reduce their hours or stop working, to cover the payment of
lost hours. However, the subsidy is very low, pushing workers to return to their jobs
too soon. In Spain, the government extended the Covid-19 unemployment benefit to
this sector; their first inclusion in provisions of unemployment benefits in the country. In Italy, the government extended a monthly cash-transfer called 'Emergency
Income' to domestic and care workers – although the amount was lower than that of
other workers. The Italian context is noteworthy too for having taken the initiative
to launch a regularization of undocumented workers in the sector. Covid-19 was
also acknowledged as a work-related injury, that is, as a possible motivation for
monetary compensation in cases where workers' infection can be demonstrated as
having arisen from contact at the homes of their employers (Marchetti &
Mesiäislehto, 2022). In brief, the condition of migrant domestic and care workers
during the pandemic can be seen as the result of the different ways in which the
policy fields of migration, on the one hand, and of labour market regulations, on the
other, intersect in each country.

References

Ally, S. (2009). *From servants to workers: South African domestic workers and the democratic
state*. Cornell University Press.
Ambrosini, M. (2015). Employers as 'care managers': Contracts, emotions and mutual obligations
within Italy's invisible welfare system. In A. Triandafyllidou & S. Marchetti (Eds.), *Paying for
care: The employers' perspective on migrant domestic work* (pp. 17–34). Ashgate.
Anderson, B. (2000). *Doing the dirty work? The global politics of domestic labour*. Zed Books.
Anderson, B. (2014). Nations, migration and domestic labour: The case of the UK. *Women's
Studies International Forum, 46*, 5–12.
Arnado, J. M. (2003). Maternalism in mistress-maid relations: The Philippine experience. *Journal
of International Women's Studies, 4*(3), 154–177.
Barua, P., Waldrop, A., & Haukanes, H. (2017). From benevolent maternalism to the market logic:
Exploring discursive boundary making in domestic work relations in India. *Critical Asian
Studies, 49*(4), 481–500.
Bauböck, R. (2011). Temporary migrants, partial citizenship and Hypermigration. *Critical Review
of International Social and Political Philosophy, 14*(5), 665–693.
Boccagni, P., & Ambrosini, M. (2012). *Cercando il benessere nelle migrazioni: L'esperienza delle
assistenti familiari straniere in Trentino*. FrancoAngeli.
Bonifazi, C., & Marini, C. (2013). The impact of the economic crisis on foreigners in the Italian
labour market. *Journal of Ethnic and Migration Studies, 40*(3), 1–19.

Boris, E., Fish, J., Garofalo Geymonat, G., & Marchetti, S. (Eds.). (2018). Beyond 'maids and madams': can employers be allies in new policies for domestic workers' rights?' *Open Democracy*. Available at https://www.opendemocracy.net/en/beyond-trafficking-and-slavery/beyond-maids-and-madams-can-em. Last accessed on 25 Oct 2020.

Bosniak, L. (2008). *The citizen and the alien: Dilemmas of contemporary membership*. University Press.

Cock, J. (1989). *Maids and madams: Domestic workers under apartheid*. Women's Press.

Collins, P. H., & Bilge, S. (2020). *Intersectionality* (2nd ed.). Polity Press.

Constable, N. (2009). Migrant workers and the many states of protest in Hong Kong. *Critical Asian Studies, 41*, 143–164.

Cretan, R., & Light, D. (2020). COVID-19 in Romania: Transnational labour, geopolitics, and the Roma 'outsiders'. *Eurasian Geography and Economics, 61*(4–5), 559–572.

Di Bartolomeo, A., & Marchetti, S. (2016). Migrant women's employment in paid reproductive work through the crisis: The case of Italy (2007–2012). *Investigaciones Feministas, 7*(1), 57–74.

Douglas, M., & Isherwood, B. C. (1979). *The worlds of goods*. Routledge.

Farris, S. (2015). Migrants' regular Army of labour: Gender dimensions of the impact of the global economic crisis on migrant labour in Western Europe. *The Sociological Review, 63*(1), 121–143.

Fraser, N. (2003). Social justice in the age of identity politics: Redistribution, recognition and participation. In N. Fraser & A. Honneth (Eds.), *Redistribution or recognition? A political-philosophical exchange*. Verso.

Goñalons-Pons, P. (2015). Modern domesticity: Why professional women hire domestic workers in Spain. In A. Triandafyllidou & S. Marchetti (Eds.), *Employers, agencies and immigration: Paying for care* (pp. 35–51). Ashgate.

Gregson, N., & Lowe, M. (1994). *Servicing the middle classes: Class, gender and waged domestic work in contemporary Britain*. Routledge.

Gutiérrez-Rodríguez, E. (2010). *Migration, domestic work and affect: A Decolonial approach on value and the feminization of labour*. Routledge.

Hall, T., & Williamson, H. (1999). *Citizenship and community*. Youth Work Press.

Haskins, V. (2001). On the doorstep: Aboriginal domestic service as a 'contact zone'. *Australian Feminist Studies, 16*(34), 13–25.

ILO. (2011). *Convention concerning decent work for domestic workers* (Vol. n. C189). ILO.

ILO. (2020). *Impact of the COVID-19 crisis on loss of jobs and hours among domestic workers*. ILO. Available at https://www.ilo.org/wcmsp5/groups/public/%2D%2D-ed_protect/%2D%2D-protrav/%2D%2D-travail/documents/publication/wcms_747961.pdf. Last accessed on 25 Oct 2020.

Isin, E. F., & Nielsen, G. M. (2008). *Acts of citizenship*. Zed Books.

Isin, E. F., Nyers, P., & Turner, B. S. (2013). *Citizenship between past and future*. Taylor & Francis.

ISTAT. (2013). *Rapporto Annuale 2013*. ISTAT.

Joppke, C. (2007). Transformation of citizenship: Status, rights, identity. *Citizenship Studies, 11*(1), 37–48.

Kaplan, E. (1987). 'I Don't do no windows': Competition between the domestic worker and the housewife. In V. Miner & H. E. Longino (Eds.), *Competition: A feminist taboo*. The Feminist Press.

Kofman, E. (2005). Citizenship, migration and the reassertion of National Identity. *Citizenship Studies, 9*(5), 453–467.

Kristeva, J. (1980). *Pouvoirs de l'horreur: Essai sur l'abjection*. Édition du Seuil.

Kuhlmann, E., Falkenbach, M., Klasa, K., Pavolini, E., Ungureanu, M. I., & M.I. (2020). Migrant carers in Europe in times of COVID-19: A call to action for European health workforce governance and a public health approach. *European Journal of Public Health, 30*(4), iv22–iv27.

Lan, P. C. (2006). *Global Cinderellas: Migrant domestic workers and newly rich employers in Taiwan*. Duke University Press.

Leiblfinger, M., Prieler, V., Schwiter, K., Steiner, J., Benazha, A., & Lutz, H. (2020). Impact of the COVID-19 pandemic on live-in care workers in Germany, Austria, and Switzerland. *LTC Responses to Covid-19*. Available at https://ltccovid.org/2020/05/14/impact-of-the-covid-19-pandemic-on-live-in-care-workers-in-germany-austria-and-switzerland/. Last accessed on 28 Oct 2020.

Leichsenring, K., Staflinger, H., & Bauer, A. (2020). The situation of '24-hour care' from the perspective of migrant caregivers in Austria. *LTC Responses to Covid-19*. Available at https://ltccovid.org/2020/04/08/the-situation-of-24-hour-care-from-the-perspective-of-migrant-caregivers-in-austria/. Last accessed on 28 Oct 2020.

Leslie, D. A. (1993). Femininity, post-fordism and new traditionalism. *Environment and Planning D: Society and Space, 11*, 689–708.

Lim, J. Y. (2000). The effects of the east Asian crisis on the employment of women and men: The Philippine case. *World Development, 28*(7), 1285–1306.

Lister, R., et al. (2007). *Gendering citizenship in Western Europe: New challenges for citizenship research in a cross-National Context*. Policy.

Locher-Scholten, E. (2000). *Women and the colonial state: Essays on gender and modernity in the Netherlands indies, 1900–1942*. University Press.

Lutz, H. (2011). *The new maids: Transnational women and the care economy*. Zed Books.

Lutz, H., Vivar, M. T. H., & Supik, L. (Eds.). (2016). *Framing intersectionality: Debates on a multi-faceted concept in gender studies*. Routledge.

Marchetti, S. (2014). *Black girls: Migrant domestic workers and colonial legacies*. Brill.

Marchetti, S. (2016). Citizenship and Maternalism in migrant domestic labour: Filipina workers and their employers in Amsterdam and Rome. In B. Gullikstad, G. K. Kristensen, & P. Ringrose (Eds.), *Paid migrant domestic labour in a changing Europe* (pp. 147–168). Palgrave Macmillan.

Marchetti, S., & Boris, E. (2020). Migrant domestic and care workers: High risk but low protection. *Open Democracy*. Available at https://www.opendemocracy.net/en/pandemic-border/migrant-domestic-and-care-workers-high-risk-low-protection/. Last accessed on 25 Oct 2020.

Marchetti, S., & Mesiäislehto, M. (2022). Migrants in Europe's domestic and care sector: The institutional response. In M. Duffy et al. (Eds.), *From crisis to catastrophe: Care, COVID-19, and pathways to change*. Rutgers University Press.

Masi de Casanova, E., Rodriguez, L., & Roldán, R. B. (2018). Informed but insecure: Employment conditions and social protection among paid domestic Workers in Guayaquil. *Latin American Perspectives, 45*(1), 163–174.

Mezzadra, S. (2006). *Diritto di fuga: Migrazioni, cittadinanza, globalizzazione*. Ombre Corte.

Milkman, R. (1976). Women's work and economic crisis: Some lessons of the great depression. *Review of Radical Political Economics, 8*(1), 73–97.

Mosse, G. (1985). *Nationalism and sexuality*. Fertig.

Mouffe, C. (1992). Feminism, citizenship and radical democratic politics. In J. Butler & J. W. Scott (Eds.), *Feminists theorize the political*. Routledge.

Mutler, A. (2020). Romanian migrants get COVID-19 as pandemic exposes bad conditions for East European Workers". *Radio Free Europe/Radio Liberty*, 30 May 2020. Available at https://www.rferl.org/a/romanian-migrants-get-covid-19-as-pandemic-exposes-bad-conditions-for-east-european-workers/30643195.html#:~:text=Hundreds%20of%20Romanian%20workers%20staged,they%20were%20working%20went%20bankrupt. Last accessed on 28 Oct 2020.

Nakano Glenn, E. (1996). From servitude to service work: Historical continuities in the racial division of paid reproductive labour. In C. L. MacDonald & C. Sirianni (Eds.), *Working in the service society* (pp. 115–156). Temple University Press.

Näre, L. (2012). Moral encounters: Drawing boundaries of class, sexuality and migrancy in paid domestic work. *Ethnic and Racial Studies, 37*(2), 363–380.

Ong, A. (1999). *Flexible citizenship: The cultural logics of Transnationality*. Duke University Press.

Ong, A. (2006). *Neoliberalism as exception: Mutations in citizenship and sovereignty*. Duke University Press.

Palmer, P. (1983). White women/black women: The dualism of female identity and experience in the United States. *Feminist Studies, 9*(1), 151–170.

Palmer, P. (1989). *Domesticity and dirt: Housewives and domestic servants in the United States, 1920–1945*. Temple University Press.

Parreñas, R. S. (2001). *Servants of globalization: Women, migration and domestic work*. Stanford University Press.

Pasquinelli, S., & Rusmini, G. (Eds.). (2013). *Badare non basta. Il lavoro di cura: 22 attori, progetti, politiche*. Ediesse.

Pastore, F., Salis, E., & Villosio, C. (2013). L'Italia e l'immigrazione lowcost: fine di un ciclo? *Mondi Migranti, 1*, 151–172.

Ray, R., & Qayum, S. (2009). *Cultures of servitude: Modernity, domesticity, and class in India*. Stanford University Press.

Reyneri, E. (2010). L'impatto della crisi sull'inserimento degli immigrati nel mercato del lavoro dell'Italia e degli altri paesi dell'Europa meridionale. *PRISMA Economia-Società-Lavoro, 2*(2), 1–17.

Ribeiro Corossacz, V. (2018). *White middle-class men in Rio de Janeiro: The making of a dominant subject*. Lexington Books.

Rollins, J. (1985). *Between women: Domestics and their employers*. Temple University Press.

Romero, M. (1992). *Maids in the USA*. Routledge.

Romero, M. (2017). *Introducing intersectionality*. Wiley.

Rosińska, A., & Pellerito, E. (2022). Pandemic shock absorbers: Domestic workers' activism at the intersection of immigrants' and workers' rights. In A. Triandafyllidou (Ed.), *Migration and pandemics*. Springer.

Rothenberg, P. (2000). *Invisible privilege: A memory about race, class and gender*. University Press of Kansas.

Rubery, J., & Rafferty, A. (2013). Women and recession revisited. *Work, Employment & Society, 27*(3), 414–432.

Sarti, R. (2005). Freedom and citizenship? The legal status of servants and domestic workers in a comparative perspective (16th–21st centuries). In S. Pasleau & I. Schopp (Eds.), *Proceedings of the servant project* (Vol. 3, pp. 127–164).

Semenza, R. (2012). Le conseguenze della crisi sull'occupazione femminile. *Il Mulino, 61*(5), 842–848.

Sharpe, J. (2003). *Ghosts of slavery: A literary archaeology of black Women's lives*. University of Minnesota Press.

Triandafyllidou, A. (2013). *Irregular migrant domestic Workers in Europe: Who cares?* Ashgate.

Triandafyllidou, A., & Marchetti, S. (Eds.). (2015). *Employers, agencies and immigration: Care work in Europe*. Ashgate.

Young, I. M. (1990). *Justice and the politics of difference*. Princeton University Press.

Yuval-Davis, N. (1999). The 'multi-layered citizen'. *International Feminist Journal of Politics, 1*(1), 119–136.

Chapter 5
Rights

5.1 Migrant Domestic Work and Rights Issues

Transnational migration gives rise to multiple forms of potential exploitation of paid domestic work, being an occupation that is relegated to the informal labour market where migrant women often find themselves in powerless positions in relation to their employers and host society. This is especially so when they are undocumented migrants, as is the case for migrants who do not fulfil the requirements for labour or family migration. As a consequence, in many countries, migrants' employment in private households is strongly deregulated and workers do not have access to social and labour protection (Triandafyllidou & Marchetti, 2017). In several countries, domestic work is not recognized as work, and is therefore excluded from labour protections. Domestic workers are often deprived of monetary payment and compensated with only food and shelter. Also, in countries where domestic work is regulated through labour laws, provisions differ significantly from those in place for other jobs, having lower remuneration and fewer social protections. This lack of a normative framework adds to the vulnerability that is typical of the sector due to the isolation that is characteristic of this kind of work (especially for live-in workers) and the social stigmatization that they face in different parts of the world.

The exploitation of domestic workers has come to be seen as a global problem whose governance is a challenge that exceeds national borders. There has been a gradual development of what can be seen as the 'global governance of paid domestic work': a multi-layered framework aimed at improving domestic workers' rights, developed by some of the key actors at the forefront of gender and migration issues in recent years. This process intensified after the promulgation in 2011 of ILO Convention 189 (C189) *Concerning Decent Work for Domestic Workers*, and the related Recommendation 201. The two documents promote not only the equal treatment of care workers in labour and employment, but also the improvement of their social status.

S. Marchetti, *Migration and Domestic Work*, IMISCOE Research Series,
https://doi.org/10.1007/978-3-031-11466-3_5

It is interesting to look at the transformation of the domestic workers' movements for labour rights into a 'global movement' and thus consider the interplay between the international actors – international institutions, governments, regional and national organizations – that have shaped this process. It is important to investigate what has motivated their increasing concern for the situation of domestic workers – a marginalized social group whose interests were seldom considered of any importance before. In fact, the ILO had already passed a resolution in 1948 demanding minimum standards for the sector (see Boris & Fish, 2015; Schwenken et al., 2011). However, attention for the plight of domestic workers gradually faded. In the post-war period it was commonly believed that the increasing modernization of domestic life, with the use of technology and more efficient systems to organize the household, would soon make it possible to spontaneously eliminate the traditional figure of the paid domestic worker, seen as a legacy of pre-modern and exploitative times (see Coser, 1973). There would no longer be any need for political intervention. It was only in the 1990s, when the ILO started its general campaign for the promotion of 'decent work' for flexible, informal and non-standard jobs, that the issue of paid domestic work came up again.

When in 2008 the ILO decided to put what would later become C189 on the agenda of their next assemblies, this immediately prefigured the possibility of a revolutionary shift. For many, it was incredible to think of a convention for a sector which traditionally suffered from an immense lack of rights, and for a kind of work that was not even recognized as such in most countries. Where it was recognized, it was given a second-rate position, as not 'real' work. After gathering the opinions of experts and activists, the ILO suggested that domestic workers should be treated as other workers in their respective countries. Equality was conceived in terms of salary but also protection in the workplace. Expanded labour rights had to be accompanied by the creation of new forms of association, and when possible, trade unions formed by domestic workers themselves. These legal and socio-political transformations could not happen without a cultural change at the level of these workers' social representation to counter the stigma attached to them. In this way, the convention combined the fight for the specific cause of domestic workers' labour rights with a wider struggle for the human rights of particularly vulnerable subjects, from undocumented migrants, to low-caste and racialized women. It is indeed this capacity of C189 to include previously invisible subjects that makes it a perfect case for a 'new right', meaning the rights recognition for social groups and minorities which were previously not even deemed to figure on the landscape of political subjects in a given context (Bob, 2011).

Since the promulgation of C189, the case of paid domestic workers has gradually emerged as a matter of political debate involving growing numbers of international actors, attracted by the emergence of domestic workers' rights as an increasingly significant policy issue at the global level. Actors who had already been involved found new legitimation. As a result, in these years we see a large range of actors become part of this field, from political parties, trade unions and grassroots workers' groups, to humanitarian NGOs, religious organizations and international organizations for workers' rights such as the International Trade Union Confederation (ITUC) and the WIEGO network. International bodies such as the ILO, the International Organization for Migration (IOM), the Global Forum on Migration and Development (GFMD), UN Women, the Commission on the Status of Women, and the European Fundamental Rights Agency are also involved (Fish, 2017; Garofalo Geymonat et al., 2017). Finally, the founding of the IDWF (previously the International Domestic Workers' Network) in Montevideo in 2013 is a clear sign of a global expansion of the movement thanks to new connections between existing national and regional organizations led by domestic workers, as in the case of CONLATRAHO[1] in Latin America.

In Europe, the European Parliament voted for the first time on a resolution for the rights of women domestic workers and carers. The proposal was made by the Greek member Kostadinka Kuneva who builds on her long-standing experience as an activist for the rights of cleaners and domestic workers in Greece. This resolution was a historical step towards equal rights for this category of workers in the framework of C189, which has thus far only been ratified by six EU Countries. For the two groups that comprise this category of workers, i.e. women and low-skilled migrants, the resolution represents an opportunity to escape their invisible condition. The European Parliament Resolution 'Women domestic workers and carers in the EU' of 2016 also emphasizes the importance of protecting workers in this sector against abuse and lack of social and legal recognition. More recently, the European Economic and Social Committee has published a report on live-in care workers in selected EU countries (the UK, Germany, Italy and Poland), supporting the request for more protection and labour rights (Rogalewski and Florel 2020).

The historical roots of C189 can be identified in other ILO campaigns for the promotion of decent work in flexible, non-standard and low-skilled informal sectors as well as in the multiple debates on women's and migrants' work that have animated the ILO agenda since the 1990s (Boris & Fish, 2014; Kott & Droux, 2013; Schwenken et al., 2011). Promoting decent work also appeals to human rights principles as is clearly reflected in C189, whose main prescription of equal labour rights for domestic workers is accompanied by a demand for recognition of their dignity as human beings (Garofalo Geymonat et al., 2017; Marchetti, 2018). Moreover, C189 incorporates an intersectional approach, appealing simultaneously to issues of gender, race, ethnicity, religious and class-based discrimination at work, and advocating for the protection of the most vulnerable categories of domestic workers, with particular reference to migrant workers (Fish, 2017; Schwenken, 2013).

---

[1] Confederación Latinoamericana y del Caribe de Trabajadoras del Hogar/Confederation of Household Workers in the Caribbean and Latin America.

5.2   Global Rights and Local Struggles

It is important to consider the impact of C189 on campaigns for domestic workers' rights waged in different national contexts. In fact, when one gets closer to the specificities of each country, there are important differences in the behaviour of social movements, states and international organizations in relation to this issue.

State and non-state organizations position themselves around the issue in contrasting ways depending on the national context and the capacity of C189 to mobilize actors in each place. This raises questions such as: how are different local actors reacting to C189 as a global governance measure for domestic workers' rights? What role does the state play in this process? How do such processes relate to wider political and social transformations taking place at the national and regional levels?

At local levels, the literature indicates a diversity of actors and objectives involved in the struggle around the C189 process. Depending on the country, several institutional and non-institutional actors may enter this field, either supporting or countering the aim of improving domestic workers' conditions. Besides domestic workers' grassroots organizations and trade unions, these actors may encompass other civil society organizations, such as general trade unions and workers' organizations (Boris & Nadasen, 2008; Chun & Cranford, 2018), women's and feminist groups, anti-racist and ethnic minority associations (Bernardino-Costa, 2014) and humanitarian NGOs (Chun & Kim, 2018). Studies have also considered organizations representing employers' interests (Chien, 2018), governmental bodies, state institutions and international organizations (Blofield, 2012).

Mobilization around C189 has been considered a paradigmatic example of the scaling up of local and national movements and the formation of the IDWF as transnational collective actor: for instance, studies have described the key role played by the International Domestic Workers' Network and by some regional and national organizations in the drafting of the convention in Geneva in 2011 (Acciari, 2019; Fish, 2017; Schwenken, 2016). Louisa Acciari (2019) suggests that this process is an example of the ability of 'subaltern groups' from the Global South to generalize their demands and produce new rights.

Some scholars have focused on the legal advances brought about by signing the convention into national laws (Albin & Mantouvalou, 2012; Du Toit, 2011; Gallotti & Mertens, 2013; Rosewarne, 2013; Viesel, 2013), while others have looked at the impact of C189 on national or regional social movements and on the political processes related to the campaigns for its ratification and subsequent implementation (Blofield & Jokela, 2018; Cherubini et al., 2020; Marchetti, 2018; Schwenken, 2013).

For many countries, the promulgation of C189 can be considered an 'external event' which has determined what Fligstein and McAdam (2012) would call an 'exogenous change' that has led to the improvement of domestic workers' rights in various countries. This type of change has provoked an important reorganization of the actors involved, the focus of their action, the alliances they establish, and the discursive frameworks that are activated.- This has determined the positive progression towards the achievement of a common goal (i.e. the improvement of domestic workers' rights). The numerous transformations that have taken place since 2008 (when the ILO put the issue on its agenda) show more generally how a policy process taking place at the international level is reflected on the national one. In other words, we see how the interconnection between 'global' and 'local' struggles can take shape. The actions and discourses used at national level will be different depending on the local political, cultural and socio-economic context. The actors which emerge as the most influential at the local level can create the conditions for an international policy to be transferred, negotiated, modified or strengthened – but also ignored or rejected – in each country. Depending on this, C189 as a tool of global governance of domestic workers' rights has been incorporated, fuelled or resisted by both state and non-state actors, depending on the country.

The way the struggle for domestic workers' rights is perceived at large determines the response to C189 to great extent. An important element to explain these different tendencies is the way the struggle for domestic workers' rights is perceived by society at large. In fact, the effectiveness of the C189 process seems to increase in countries where improving the condition of domestic workers is seen as emblematic of a social justice struggle valid for the entire country (Marchetti et al., 2021). Conversely, in countries where domestic workers are easily associated with 'others' from outside the nation, the campaign remains isolated and issue-specific, and it is difficult for activists to build a large consensus beyond direct stakeholders on domestic workers' issues. In other words, the global rights of domestic workers are more easily promoted at the national level when they are seen as part of a wider political project for social justice. Conversely, in those contexts where the connection with wider political struggles is weaker or absent, the question of domestic workers' rights is framed more narrowly as a policy issue, rather than political. In those contexts, giving more rights to this category was not meant to challenge the structural factors shaping this sector and the exploitation therein.

5.3 Domestic Workers' Organizing

Self-organized groups of domestic workers – trade unions, associations and networks composed of and led by women employed in the sector – have emerged as prominent across all countries in the politicization of domestic workers' struggle for rights. Some early examples from South African (Ally 2009, Fish, 2017) domestic workers' organizing are noteworthy as a form of collective action to fight simultaneously for labour rights, human dignity and social recognition.

At the global level, these organizations seek to represent the interests of multiply-marginalized social groups that are employed in the sector worldwide, namely migrants, low-class, low-status, racialized, and rural, girls and women. Thus, domestic workers' mobilizations often offer a space where several usually separate social struggles converge, such as those for equal labour rights and class equity, women's rights, recognition for ethnic and racialized minorities, and migrants' rights. This may make room for solidarity, coalitions and alliances across different social movements and political projects (Marchetti et al., 2021).

A comparative assessment of the strategies adopted by domestic workers' organizations in Colombia, Brazil, Ecuador, Italy, Spain, Germany, Philippines, Taiwan and India in the struggle for domestic workers' rights reveals how these intersections work in action. We see that the strategies change depending on the national socio-economic, cultural and political context. Interestingly, one of the major discursive frameworks used by advocates of domestic workers' rights recuperates the argument on the transnational commodification of care discussed in Chap. 2 of this book. This discourse plays on the connection between migrants' exploitation in this sector and the crisis of welfare states in industrialized ageing societies. It is thus especially common among interviewees in Italy, Spain, Germany and Taiwan as destination countries for migrants in the elder care sector. In other words, this framework is a critique of marketized forms of care provision and the reliance of states on foreign labour recruitment.

Moreover, during the time of the campaign for C189 ratification, Brazilian activists – in particular from the national federation FENATRAD[2] – mobilized rhetorical devices which show how racism towards black domestic workers is a continuation of the attitudes that existed under slavery. In this way they established a connection with the legacy of the anti-racist movement in the country. In Colombia, the Afro-Colombian domestic workers' union UTRASD[3] employed an intersectional discursive repertoire in which domestic work is addressed as a simultaneously gendered, class-based and racialized activity. The specific experience lived by Afro-Colombian women, especially internal migrants and refugees, is at the heart of UTRASD's identity in their recurrent self-identification as 'the first ethnic-based domestic workers' union in the country'. In Ecuador, the configuration is slightly different: race-based discrimination is recognized as an additional burden, but not as an intrinsic feature of the social organization of domestic work and of the collective identity promoted by the movement. In particular, the activists of the domestic workers' association ATRH[4] appear to see the category of 'organized Ecuadorian domestic workers' as mainly shaped by the interplay of gender and class inequalities.

A different scenario emerges when we consider the demands and actions of these groups. These can be summarized in the following instances. First of all, many of the activist groups employ sensitization activities promoting the motto 'domestic work is work', thus asking for changes in the legal framework, but also radical socio-economic changes which may raise the conditions of domestic workers more generally. These campaigns are largely aimed at demanding recognition for

---

[2] Federação Nacional das Trabalhadoras Domésticas (National Federation of Domestic Workers, Brazil).

[3] Unión de Trabajadoras Afrocolombianas del Servicio Doméstico (Afro-Colombian Domestic Workers' Trade Union, Colombia)

[4] Asociación de Trabajadoras Remuneradas de Hogar (Association of Paid Domestic Workers, Ecuador)

domestic work with the argument that decent work deserves equal rights, the same claim that is central to the discourse deployed by the ILO and the other international organizations involved in the global governance of domestic work.

At the same time, one strategy used by organizations consists of interventions in the use of language both in public discourse and in everyday interactions (ibid.). In fact, most of the organizations have engaged in debates about an adequate name to address domestic workers. Refusing the diminishing terms commonly used in their local languages, they seek legitimacy for the new identity created by the movement as workers performing a valuable job and as bearers of rights. This challenges the representations of domestic work as 'intimate' yet 'dirty' work that are often internalized by workers themselves, to the point where workers are not even 'out' to their own parents or children, such as occurs in India. There are cases in which the family remains central to the semantic activist innovation, such as in the Philippines with *kasambahay* (companion in the family) and in Italy with *colf* (*collaboratrice familiare*, collaborator of the family). Yet even these new terms have the effect of challenging the ambivalent position of the worker within the employing family, where they had traditionally been 'part of the family' – if subordinate.

The capacity of domestic workers' groups to carry out empowering activities for their members and for domestic workers as a whole is another striking aspect of their activism (ibid.). We see that many organizations offer a host of services and education. In addition to legal support, information on job contracts, working conditions and professional training, they also provide schooling and literacy programs, education against gender-based violence and for women's health and wellbeing, and political and leadership training. The latter are designed to strengthen knowledge and abilities that are key to active participation in the public and political sphere (for example strategies for unionization or public speaking). Some of the organizations have set up plans for improving the economic conditions and bargaining power of their members, through the creation of community saving cooperatives or domestic workers' cooperatives. Depending on the circumstances and opportunities in the field, some of these activities and programmes were created and delivered autonomously from the bottom, while others happened in collaboration with allies (both non-profit organizations and public institutions). As a whole, we see how these organizations also function as solidarity and mutual support groups that support domestic workers both in their labour relations and in other aspects of their lives.

To sum up, the movement is characterized by special forms of labour and women's organizing, where mobilizing for labour rights and political pressure towards institutional actors go hand in hand with cultural politics. This also addresses the importance of self-representation, self-esteem and identity. In other words, the function of these groups transcends the field of labour alone and expands towards wider issues related to women's experiences, migration, access to education, political participation, personal and economic autonomy, as well as health, sexuality, and personal and family wellbeing.

5.4   Not Such Easy Allies for Domestic Workers

If, seen from one side, the domestic workers' movement has some very unique characteristics, from the other it can be seen as having somewhat of a shared composition and similar goals to certain other social movements. Depending on the context,
these can be groups defending the rights of women and girls in general, racialized
people and minorities, migrants and undocumented people, or workers in the service and informal sectors. However, these overlaps and convergences do not neces-
sarily lead to easy and spontaneous alliances between domestic workers and other
organizations, and difficulties often arise when organizers engage in alliance making. In this part, I will discuss these difficulties in two exemplary cases: alliances
with trade unions and with feminist groups.

Firstly, it is important to understand the role of traditional trade unions in the
struggle to assert the rights of migrant domestic workers. There has been intense
discussion on the relationship between migrants and labour organizations (Penninx
& Roosblad, 2000; Wets, 2000). Viewed negatively, as Lucio and Perrett (2009)
argue, migration puts under threat the very identity of labour organizations, asking
them to redefine their purpose to include foreign workers' issues. It also requires the
formulation of specific anti-discrimination policies that are necessary for equal
opportunities in the labour market (Verbeek & Penninx, 2009; Watts, 2002), and
that they overcome an absence of sensitivity towards racial discrimination within
the labour organizations themselves (Lucio & Perrett, 2009). In all these matters,
scholars agree that it is extremely important to consider the regional differences
concerning, simultaneously, the characteristics of the predominant migrant population, the cultural context in which they arrive, and the traditions of the organizations
established there (Penninx & Roosblad, 2000, p. 200).

With the purpose of an intra-European comparison, Rinus Penninx and Judith
Roosblad have organized this discussion into three main questions (2000, pp. 4–11).
These correspond in their view to the 'dilemmas' that trade unions have historically
faced in relation to foreign labour forces. The first dilemma concerns the backbone
of the relation between labour organizations and migration by asking if labour organizations have to accept, or even encourage, the employment of foreign workers. It
is true that the arrival of cheap labour from outside might undermine the rights of
national workers. Yet, although in a different form, this question is today newly
relevant as labour organizations have to position themselves on government labour
migration policies. Once migrant workers are actually employed in the national
labour market, a second dilemma arises: what kind of membership can migrant
workers have in the national labour organizations? Are they going to join national
workers, or should separate organizations be established for their interests alone?
The third dilemma is also the most complex: once migrants are included in labour
organizations' strategies, how should they be treated? In other words, should the
organizations side with the foreign workers, demanding a different treatment for
them at the workplace? This has been called the 'equal-versus-different-dilemma'
and is considered the most insidious.

When it comes to feminist organizations, it is worth noting that they are only rarely directly engaged in struggles for domestic workers' rights, and the conceptual linkages that we see do not automatically correspond to forms of alliance between the two movements. As is the case for other women activists who mobilize for workers' rights or against social marginalization, domestic workers' groups are often reluctant to define themselves as feminist. In fact, the perception of distance from the feminist movement is a recurrent topic in the accounts of domestic workers' activists across different national contexts and time periods. The complicated relationship between domestic workers' rights activism and feminist activism is worth exploring to understand the conditions that make it possible in certain countries to have feminist organizations allied with domestic workers' rights, and not in others. To understand this diversity we have to take into account the different feminist traditions in each country, the other actors involved in domestic workers' rights, and importantly, the discursive frameworks that have been mobilized to promote them.

It can be argued that in spite of the disconnection that exists in many contexts between these two movements at the practical level, they share a great deal in their common critique of contemporary capitalist society and its exploitation of women, migrants and domestic workers (Marchetti et al., 2021). We find that at the level of discourse, feminist arguments are widely represented in this field, with activists for domestic workers' rights incorporating the classic repertoire of feminist critique into their own narratives. In particular, activists recurrently speak of the rights of paid domestic workers within a broader view on feminist and anti-capitalist critiques of inequality and exploitation of women's work.

The feminist argument on the valorization of reproductive labour (see Chap. 2 of this book) is widely used by domestic workers' rights advocates when they talk about how their countries should recognize the value of their work, starting from appreciating the reproductive labour done by women inside their own homes and families. In other words, as they claim the recognition of 'domestic work as work', they not only demand the right to contracts, better salaries and labour protection for themselves, but also challenge the general devaluation of all tasks connected with caregiving and housekeeping. However, they also modify and expand this traditional feminist argument, which was developed around unpaid labour, to include the case of paid workers, and their experiences of discrimination and exploitation both as women and people who belong to low-class, ethnic, racialized and caste minorities (ibid.).

In countries where, by contrast, the majority of domestic workers are migrant caregivers for elderly people, we observe a more frequent use of another feminist framework relating to the commodification of care, which in turn connects to feminist critiques of welfare systems and the care crisis. It is worth pointing out that in these contexts, some of the actors involved in the field of domestic workers' rights that have emerged in the last decade in particular are those representing care receivers and employers' needs, and their motivation at least partly taps into the debate on the commodification of care. Class differences in these contexts are complicated by the fact that employers belong to a whole range of social positions, including those with lower incomes, for whom hiring a home-based caregiver is often the only option given the lack of support from the state for elderly, chronically ill and disabled people. In this context, domestic workers' activists tend to expand feminist arguments on care and welfare issues by placing migrants at the centre, and arguing that migrants bear the burden of the limited social provisions in the Global North.

Finally, it is important to highlight how in these different appropriations of feminist frameworks, domestic workers' activists enact a transformation of these arguments in what can be seen as an intersectional perspective. Indeed, they expand the capacity of these arguments so as to include racialized, low-class, migrant and other minority groups in ways few feminist movements have achieved. In other words, domestic workers' activists tend to create a larger inclusive discourse to promote domestic workers' rights through intersectionality. This capacity can be seen as a creative force within the domestic workers' movement, which may facilitate the building of alliances with other groups for domestic workers' interests, but also to expand the scope of contemporary feminisms (Box 5.1).

Box 5.1: The Impact of C189 in Nine Countries

During the period 2008–18, **in Ecuador** and the **Philippines** there was a strong synergy between the ILO, national governments, and civil society actors, including domestic workers' groups (Marchetti et al., 2021). The state was quick to ratify C189 and legislative measures were adopted on the basis of its requirements. Domestic workers' organizing was promoted. Other civil society actors were also responsive to the ILO campaign, taking the struggle beyond the institutional level. At the local level, C189 encountered a suitable cultural and political ground, with key collaborations between the government, NGOs, domestic workers and the local ILO office in particular, which was fully involved in the local process.

In the same period in **Colombia** and **Brazil**, there was a larger process at work (ibid.). There, a vibrant dynamism in civil society was combined with the involvement of the state and other institutional actors. The C189 process was embedded in a wider transformation process at play in the country, involving domestic workers as one of the key target groups – although not exclusively. Demands by domestic workers' groups explicitly went beyond C189, advocating for more radical changes in the conditions of domestic workers at the legislative, social and economic levels. Although C189 was the exogenous change animating the field, the legacy of past experiences is extremely relevant to understanding these contexts, since domestic workers' organizations and a long-standing tradition in workers' and women's movements were already a reality there.

In **Taiwan**, **India** and **Spain** there was a strong involvement of civil society, domestic workers' groups, and the ILO (with the exception of Taiwan for the latter) (ibid.). However, this cannot counterbalance the lack of support

(continued)

> **Box 5.1** (continued)
>
> from the government, which is of course essential to the institutional process. Domestic workers' rights were opposed not only by employers' interest groups but also by the conservative parties in power and opposing egalitarian reforms, and by brokers acting as market intermediaries whose private interests were in maintaining the status quo. In fact, domestic workers were perceived as minority subjects (lower caste and 'tribal' people in India, migrants and undocumented people in Taiwan and Spain), whose interests were not beneficial to society as a whole, and could actually conflict with the interest of the majority.
>
> Finally, during the same period, in **Italy** and **Germany** there was an observable impasse in the accomplishment of the C189 process and the full promotion of domestic workers' rights, partly due to a contradiction between a formal adherence by the state to C189 and the lack of a real implementation of C189 principles (ibid.). These countries' governments ratified C189, since their national legislation was, in their thinking, already in line with the C189 requirements. However, the ratification of C189 ought to have been followed by corresponding policy measures for a full implementation of C189 principles, which was not the case. Moreover, in these countries civil society and social movements do not mobilize on the issue of domestic workers' rights, which are largely seen as a problem concerning foreign – and often undocumented – workers.

References

Acciari, L. (2019). Decolonising labour, reclaiming subaltern epistemologies: Brazilian domestic workers and the International Struggle for Labour Rights. *Contexto Internacional, 41*(1), 39–64.

Albin, E., & Mantouvalou, V. (2012). The ILO convention on domestic workers: From the shadows to the light. *Industrial Law Journal, 41*(1), 67–78.

Ally, S. A. (2009). From servants to workers. *South African domestic workers and the democratic state*. Cornell University Press.

Bernardino-Costa, J. (2014). Intersectionality and female domestic workers' unions in Brazil. *Women's Studies International Forum, 46*(C), 72–80.

Blofield, M. (2012). *Care work and class: Domestic workers' struggle for equal rights in Latin America*. Penn State Press.

Blofield, M., & Jokela, M. (2018). Paid domestic work and the struggles of care workers in Latin America. *Current Sociology, 66*(4), 531–546.

Bob, C. (Ed.). (2011). *The international struggle for new human rights*. University of Pennsylvania Press.

Boris, E., & Fish, J. (2014). 'Slaves no more': Making global labor standards for domestic workers. *Feminist Studies, 40*(2), 411–443.

Boris, E., & Fish, J. (2015). Decent work for domestics: Feminist organizing, worker empowerment, and the ILO. In D. Hoerder, E. van Nederveen Meerkerk, & S. Neunsinger (Eds.), *Towards a global history of domestic and caregiving workers* (pp. 530–552). Brill.

Boris, E., & Nadasen, P. (2008). Domestic workers organize! *WorkingUSA: The Journal of Labor and Society, 11*(4), 413–443.

Cherubini, D., Garofalo Geymonat, G., & Marchetti, S. (2020). Intersectional politics on domestic workers' rights: The cases of Ecuador and Colombia. In E. Evans & É. Lépinard (Eds.), *Intersectionality in feminist and queer movements: Confronting privileges* (pp. 236–254). Routledge.

Chien, Y. C. (2018). The struggle for recognition: The politics of migrant care worker policies in Taiwan. *Critical Sociology, 44*(7–8), 1147–1161.

Chun, J. J., & Cranford, C. (2018). Becoming homecare workers: Chinese immigrant women and the changing worlds of work, care and unionism. *Critical Sociology, 44*(7–8), 1013–1027.

Chun, J. J., & Kim, Y.-S. (2018). Feminist entanglements with the neoliberal welfare state: NGOs and domestic worker organizing in South Korea. In R. Agarwala & J. J. Chun (Eds.), *Gendering struggles against informal and precarious work* (pp. 147–168). Emerald Publishing Limited.

Coser, L. A. (1973). Servants: The obsolescence of an occupational role. *Social Forces, 52*(1), 31–40.

Du Toit, D. (2011). Domestic workers' convention: A breakthrough in human rights. *Law, Democracy and Development, 15*(1), 4–7.

Fish, J. N. (2017). *Domestic Workers of the World Unite! A global movement for dignity and human rights*. New York University Press.

Fligstein, N., & McAdam, D. (2012). *A theory of fields*. University Press.

Gallotti, M., & Mertens, J. (2013). *Promoting integration for migrant domestic Workers in Europe: A synthesis of Belgium, France, Italy and Spain* (International migration papers no. 118). ILO. Available from https://digitalcommons.ilr.cornell.edu/intl/291

Garofalo Geymonat, G., Marchetti, S., & Kyritsis, P. (Eds.). (2017). Domestic workers speak: A global fight for rights and recognition. *Open Democracy*. Available from https://www.opendemocracy.net/en/beyond-trafficking-and-slavery/global-landscape-of-voices-for-labour-right/

Kott, S., & Droux, J. (Eds.). (2013). *Globalizing social rights: The International Labour Organization and beyond*. Palgrave Macmillan.

Lucio, M. M., & Perrett, R. (2009). The diversity and politics of trade unions' responses to minority ethnic and migrant workers: The context of the UK. *Economic and Industrial Democracy, 30*(3), 324–347.

Marchetti, S. (2018). The global governance of paid domestic work: Comparing the impact of ILO convention no. 189 in Ecuador and India. *Critical Sociology, 44*(7–8), 1191–1205.

Marchetti, S., Cherubini, D., & Garofalo Geymonat, G. (2021). *Global domestic workers: Intersectional inequalities and struggles for rights*. University Press.

Penninx, R., & Roosblad, J. (2000). *Trade unions, immigration, and immigrants in Europe, 1960–1993*. Universiteit van Amsterdam – IMES.

Rogalewski, A., & Florek, K. (2020). The future of live-in care work in Europe: Report on the EESC country visits to the United Kingdom, Germany, Italy and Poland following up on the EESC opinion on 'The rights of live-in care workers', *European Economic and Social Committee*, Brussels. Available at: https://www.eesc.europa.eu/sites/default/files/files/report_on_the_eesc_country_visits_to_uk_germany_italy_poland_0.pdf (last accessed 25 October 2020).

Rosewarne, S. C. (2013). The ILO's domestic worker convention (C189): Challenging the gendered disadvantage of Asia's foreign domestic workers? *Global Labour Journal, 4*(1), 1–25.

Schwenken, H. (2013). *Speedy Latin America, slow Europe? Regional implementation processes of the ILO convention of decent work for domestic workers*. United Nations Research Institute for Social Development. Available from http://www.unrisd.org/80256B3C005BCCF9/search/97AA08A7519A3BA9C1257D39005B8205?OpenDocument

Schwenken, H. (2016). The emergence of an impossible movement: Domestic workers organize globally. In D. Gosewinkel & D. Rucht (Eds.), *Transnational struggles for recognition: New perspectives on civil society since the twentieth century* (pp. 205–228). Berghahn.

Schwenken, H., Prügl, E., Pabon, R., Hobden, C., & Shireen, A. (2011). An ILO convention for domestic workers. *International Feminist Journal of Politics, 13*(3), 437–461.

Triandafyllidou, A., & Marchetti, S. (2017). *Employers, agencies and immigration: Paying for care*. Routledge.

Verbeek, S., & Penninx, R. (2009). Employment equity policies in work organisations. In K. Kraal, J. Roosblad, & J. Wrench (Eds.), *Equal opportunities and ethnic inequality in European Labour Markets*. Imiscoe.

Viesel, S. (2013). Who cares? The ILO convention 'decent work for domestic workers'. *Transnational Social Review, 3*(2), 229–243.

Watts, J. R. (2002). *Immigration policy and the challenge of globalization: Unions and employers in unlikely Alliance*. ILR Press.

Wets, J. (Ed.). (2000). *Cultural diversity in trade unions: A challenge to class identity?* Ashgate.

Chapter 6
Conclusion

I hope that readers of this book will have found in it a complete and inspiring overview of the many issues at stake around the topic of domestic work, from a migratory perspective. Some of the issues discussed in this volume actually go beyond the experience of migrants, in as far as they may concern the non-migrants among domestic workers. But they also concern workers in the care sectors more generally, as well as the households, companies or institutions for which they work.

In order to introduce readers to these topics, I have taken them on a journey, reviewing existing studies, summarizing the relevant developments of the scholarship, and identifying the main issues and interpretations as they have taken shape from the 1990s until the present. Along the way, readers can find examples of the conditions of domestic workers in some countries, and a discussion of the main actors and policy interventions that have characterized this field in recent years. Indeed, my aim was for the book to merge the presentation of research results and discussion of case studies with more theoretical insights surrounding the feminization of migration and the specific issue of migrant domestic work.

In the first chapters I provided a systematic overview of the most pertinent concepts and interpretations elaborated within the different streams of the scholarship on gender and migration studies. For instance, in Chap. 1, I provided a general definition of what 'domestic work' is, based in the main on the definition provided by the International Labour Organization in its Convention no. 189 on the rights of domestic workers. I also discussed the difference between the notions of the international division of reproductive labour and global care chains, which are at the heart of the relationship between gender and migration in a globalized perspective. I argued for the necessity of a multi-layered approach to the issue of migrant domestic workers, namely combining the analysis of three political regimes that act simultaneously in this field: the gender regime, the welfare regime and the migratory regime.

A major topic in this scholarship has been the question of reproductive labour, and the way it is commodified and marketized in a transnational dimension. In

© The Author(s) 2022
S. Marchetti, *Migration and Domestic Work*, IMISCOE Research Series,
https://doi.org/10.1007/978-3-031-11466-3_6

Chap. 2, I discussed the uniqueness of all work relating to the sphere of care, and the relevance of imagination and cultural realms in this respect. I thus illustrate the feminist debate on the care economy, a theme that has become increasingly influential in migration studies, when looking at the political economy of transnational migrations. Indeed, care issues emerge as a political matter, object of state policies and social tensions which change from place to place.

The role of states became central in Chap. 3. Drawing attention to the particular conditions of the many undocumented and irregular workers in this sector, I discussed the failure of European policies concerning migrant domestic work. We have seen how, at the global level, state policies tend to create ties between labour conditions and migratory status. Although the details of such regulations may be different in the various countries, in all cases subjects are kept in a situation of permanent precarity. In this regard, it is important to look at the role of private actors such as recruitment and employment agencies – or intermediaries more generally – that work transnationally, sometimes across borders. The marketization of domestic work is accompanied by the diffusion of neoliberal attitudes toward labour, which emphasize the importance of skills, personal profiles, individual mobility patterns and so forth. In this chapter I discussed the case of circular migrants, which is particularly telling not only as a mobility pattern and policy issue, but also in relation to the way care is organized and experienced in contemporary societies, both by caregivers and care receivers. I discussed the importance of social and national networks between migrant domestic workers.

To talk about all these issues ultimately leads us to talk about the inequality that affects migrant domestic workers (Chap. 4) and the struggles to improve their rights (Chap. 5). In order to understand the multiple levels of inequality that affect domestic workers, and the way these different inequalities may be intertwined, it is essential that we adopt an intersectional perspective. An intersectional view applies both to differences within the category of domestic workers, and to differences between domestic workers and other subjects. On the latter, Chap. 4 discussed the relationship between domestic workers and their (women) employers. On the former, it looks at the hierarchies at play in the 'care market' and how they apply to different groups of migrant workers depending on their age, nationality, education, and so on. In Chap. 4, I broached wider processes such as colonial legacies, citizenship entitlements, sentiments of belonging and the inheritance of past slavery, and how they have shaped and reproduced these inequalities through time. Speaking of inequality, I thought it was also important to address how two specific contextual developments may affect domestic workers: first, an economic crisis (examples are discussed from the 2008 crisis in Italy), and secondly, the outbreak of the Covid-19 pandemic, about which I provide statistical data and examples of policy interventions.

Finally, in Chap. 5 the focus was on the mobilizations for the labour rights of domestic workers that have taken place at the international level over the last couple of decades. Building on the results of the DomEQUAL project, the chapter described the development of the movements for domestic workers' rights in several countries. It looked at the role of NGOs, governments, trade unions, domestic workers' groups and migrant activism. It delved into the relationship between international and local actors. I discussed these campaigns' allies and opponents by recounting the role of traditional women's and workers' movements specifically as they relate to domestic workers. Lastly, this chapter also offered an overview of the many insights from the studies of legal and social movements towards understanding domestic workers' rights and their violations, which represent the most recent developments in the scholarship.